Deric Longden was born in Chesterfield in 1936 and married Diana Hill in 1957. They had two children, Sally and Nicholas. After various jobs Deric took over a small factory making lingerie; he began writing and broadcasting in the 1970s and before long he was writing regularly for programmes such as *Does He Take Sugar?* and *Woman's Hour*. The demands made on him by Diana's illness, subsequently believed to be a form of ME, forced Deric to sell the factory, and since then he has devoted himself to writing, broadcasting, lecturing and after-dinner speaking. *Diana's Story*, published some years after Diana's death, was a bestseller, as was its successor, *Lost for Words*. Deric Longden married the writer Aileen Armitage in 1990 and lives in Huddersfield.

Also by Deric Longden

DIANA'S STORY
LOST FOR WORDS

and published by Corgi Books

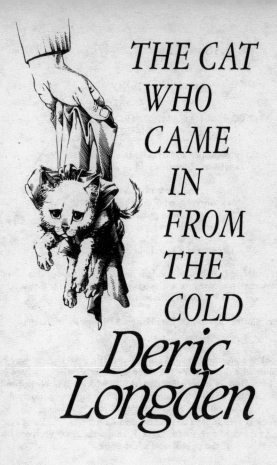

THE CAT
WHO
CAME
IN
FROM
THE
COLD
Deric Longden

CORGI BOOKS

THE CAT WHO CAME IN FROM THE COLD
A CORGI BOOK 0 552 13822 3

Originally published in Great Britain by Bantam Press,
a division of Transworld Publishers Ltd

PRINTING HISTORY
Bantam Press edition published 1991
Corgi edition published 1992
Corgi edition reprinted 1993

Copyright © Deric Longden 1991

The right of Deric Longden to be identified as the author of this work
has been asserted in accordance with sections 77 and 78 of the Copyright
Designs and Patents Act 1988.

Text illustrations by Michael Foster, Maltings Partnership

Set in 10/13pt Linotype Bembo by
Falcon Graphic Art Ltd, Wallington, Surrey.

Corgi Books are published by Transworld Publishers Ltd,
61–63 Uxbridge Road, Ealing, London W5 5SA,
in Australia by Transworld Publishers (Australia) Pty Ltd,
15–25 Helles Avenue, Moorebank, NSW 2170,
and in New Zealand by Transworld Publishers (N.Z.) Ltd,
3 William Pickering Drive, Albany, Auckland.

Printed and bound in Great Britain by
Cox & Wyman Ltd., Reading, Berks.

To Jim Cochrane and all my friends
at Transworld – for bringing *me*
in from the cold

Chapter One

If the kitten hadn't smiled up at me, well maybe I could have resisted him. Just the palest flicker moved across his serious little chess-player's face – and then it quickly dived for cover, back under the worried frown. But it was enough and in that moment he had me where he wanted me.

Patrick had introduced us over the hedge.

'What about that then?'

'What about what?'

'That – over there.'

He pointed to an upturned bucket on the top of which a small white kitten was performing a semi-professional juggling act with a wine-stained cork and a clothes-peg.

'Is it yours?'

'Yes.'

'Let's have a look at it.'

I had never thought of Patrick as an animal lover. He was a big man, as hard as nails and I didn't know then about his soft centre.

The kitten disappeared from sight as a huge fist closed over him and then he blinked at the sunlight as he emerged on my side of the hedge.

He was about the size of a jam pot and he had

a leg stuck on each corner.

'What's his name?'

'Tigger.'

'That's original.'

'It's the name he came with.'

The kitten looked up at me and shook his head as though to say it wasn't.

'There's nothing to him. What are you feeding him on?'

'He can catch mice – I don't believe in spoiling 'em.'

As dusk fell I watched him from the kitchen window. Down in the courtyard next door he sat on his bucket, a bewildered expression on his sad little face as he wondered why his mother hadn't come for him yet.

Aileen crept up silently behind me.

'You're not still worried about that kitten?'

'It's tiny. It could get mugged by a mouse.'

'We haven't got any mice.'

'Then the poor little devil's going to starve to death.'

It was out there again early next morning. Patrick and Sarah had gone to work and the kitten mooched around the courtyard sniffing at the pansies, the only flowers he could reach with such a low-slung nose.

He worked out for a few minutes on the rim of a plant pot and then went and sat on his bucket once more. Somebody had pinched his cork and his clothes-peg was clamped tight to a tea-towel as it swung on the line – it was Monday morning and the peg had a living to earn.

So had I. I took a slice of toast and a coffee into
my office and switched on the computer. This was
the best part of the day – sitting at my desk, in my
dressing-gown, reading over the pages I had written
the day before.

Out of the corner of my eye and two storeys
down, I could see the Lowry-like figures bent against
the drizzle, battling their way to work. I'd had thirty
years of that but not any more – I switched on the fan
heater with my naked toe and took a bite of toast.

Drizzle. The kitten would be getting soaked. I
pushed my chair back and then paused as common
sense tapped me on the shoulder.

'Where are you going?'

'I'm just going to have a look at the kitten – see
if it's all right.'

'How do you mean – see if it's all right?'

'It'll be getting wet.'

'It's a cat – they're waterproof for God's sake.'

'I suppose you're right.'

'Of course I'm right – so where are you going?'

'Get some more toast.'

'No you're not. You haven't finished that slice yet
– you're going to . . .'

'Oh piss off.'

He was still sitting on his upturned bucket, but he
seemed to have shrunk. With his white fur plastered
flat against his head he was only half the size he had
been and that meant there was hardly any kitten there
at all.

He looked up and caught sight of me. I quickly pulled my head away from the kitchen window. Aileen appeared at my elbow.

'What's wrong?'

Common sense could take the rest of the day off – here was the original article, in the flesh.

'It's the kitten – he's still down there.'

'What's he doing – throwing things at you?'

'No – he's just looking at me.'

'It shouldn't be allowed,' she said and switched on the kettle. I switched it off and filled it with water.

'I feel sorry for it.'

'I know you do.'

'But I don't want to get involved.'

'I know you don't.'

'You're a big help.'

'I know I am.'

I took another peep through the window and he was waiting for me. For a moment I thought he was going to wave, but no – he just smiled.

'He smiled at me.'

'He what?'

'He smiled at me.'

'Oh God.'

But he had. It was the sort of smile that suggests, 'I'm in a hell of a mess, God knows, but I can still laugh at life – well, you have to, don't you?' And then he looked away – overcome by the hopelessness of it all. Was that a tear glinting in the corner of his eye?

I pulled open the fridge door.

'What are you doing?'

'Breakfast.'

'I'll just have toast.'

'The kitten.'

'I don't believe this.'

I took out half a roast chicken and carved a slice from the breast – then another.

'One will do.'

'Yes I know, but the outside gets hard. It's softer if you take it from the inside . . . ' I tailed off, realizing how ridiculous I sounded. 'It'll only have its milk teeth,' I added, trying to justify myself.

'Then take it some milk.'

'That's a good idea.'

I cut the chicken into bite-sized chunks with the scissors and covered the pattern on a saucer with milk.

'Here.'

'What?'

Aileen held out a piece of kitchen roll.

'Take him a napkin – we don't want him spilling it all over his fur.'

I was halfway down the fifteen stone steps to the courtyard before I realized that I was still in my bare feet and dressing-gown. The drizzle was getting the hang of it now and turning into the grown-up stuff. What the hell – I was going to have a shower anyway.

'Where are you puss?'

The courtyard was surrounded by a twelve-foot-high stone wall and the hedge that separated Patrick's half from my half was matching it inch for inch.

'Come on – breakfast.'

The hedge was thicker than the wall and I had

11

to fall on my hands and knees to peer through the sparser growth down by the roots. The kitten was peering through at me from the other side – he didn't have to go down on his hands and knees.

'Good morning.'

He nodded politely.

'There you are – it's chicken.'

I tried to push the saucer through between the roots but the space wasn't wide enough, so I tilted the saucer slightly and the chicken fell off.

'Damn.'

He frowned – he wasn't used to swearing.

'Can you reach it from there?'

He was puzzled – he wasn't sure what I was up to.

'It's nearer your side than mine.'

He wasn't there – he was gone.

Where was he? I heard a lapping noise from down by my left foot and there he was, sitting on a corner of my dressing-gown – his little pink tongue dipping in and out of the saucer.

How did he do that? It was as though he had been beamed through the hedge.

'You're a clever lad.'

I bent over him and patted his head and he took off. He leapt a foot in the air, cracked me under the chin and landed in the saucer.

'I'm sorry. I didn't mean to frighten you.'

He was now sitting under a rhubarb umbrella about a yard away – his white fur punked out into sodden spikes, his prim little paws laced neatly together, his whiskers two sizes too large for him.

He had the ridiculous dignity of an elderly General who had no idea that his fly was undone.

I stood up and walked towards him. He stood up and walked away from me.

'I won't hurt you.'

I cornered him by the stone trough.

'You've got to go back home.'

There was nothing he would like better. The waterlogged fur began to rise on his back, reluctantly at first, but then sheer will-power soon had it standing to attention.

I watched his legs grow two inches longer and then he made a break for it. Dipping his shoulder and feinting to the left, he sold me the perfect dummy – zapping between the coalhouse door and a bag of fine Irish peat, he went like a racehorse across the stone pavers towards the hedge.

I sauntered across after him. There was no hurry – he was stuck between two thick privet trunks, his little back legs still pounding away and kicking up dirt like the only car in the rally without four-wheel drive.

With one hand I eased back one of the offending branches and with the other I pushed at his furry little bottom. A shiver ran all along his spine – he'd heard about men like me.

The spinning tyres suddenly gripped at the loose soil and he shot through the gap and raced towards the safety of his upturned bucket.

I bent my head and I could see him, breathing heavily atop his enamel castle.

Under my hands I felt the small chunks of chicken

and I began to flick them, Subbuteo-like, over to his side of the courtyard.

'There you are – it's chicken.'

He gave a shudder of disgust, raised one leg high in the air and began to lick his bottom. If this was breakfast – he could very well do without it.

It rained all day – well almost. Around four o'clock the weather took a tea-break and I took a stroll in the garden. Every ten minutes or so since breakfast I had indulged in a little kitten-checking from high up in the kitchen window, but now I could get a breath of fresh air and a close-up.

All day he had splashed about the courtyard chasing leaves – he didn't seem to know about cover, that it might be drier under the steps or in the porch. He would hide behind his bucket in the pouring rain, waiting for an unsuspecting leaf to stroll by, and then he would jump out and thump it.

Every now and then one of the bigger leaves would turn nasty and fight back and he would jump up on to his bucket out of harm's way. The half-inch metal rim now held a shallow pond and as he sat down he would lower his furry little bottom gingerly, a look of pure distaste wavering across his face. But it was his bucket and it was safe up there.

The leaves were a nuisance – even the pleasant ones. Within minutes of being cast off by the trees in Greenhead Park, they would band together and then rush across the road to block our drains and beat up poor defenceless kittens.

I decided to teach them a lesson and nipped into

the cellar for a brush and a shovel. Ten steps lead down to the cellar, then there's a twist under a stone porch before the door comes into view.

The porch is where the leaves go to die. Thousands of them lay face up, on their backs, legs in the air – silently willing themselves into peat.

I made a start there, and I had the best part of a bin-liner full before I began work on the steps. As I stood on the third from the bottom my head emerged above the level of the courtyard, and through the hedge I could see a little white face wondering where the hell I'd got to.

'I'm clearing up the leaves,' I told him.

'Serves 'em right.'

'They're a nuisance aren't they?'

'One bit me.'

He watched with interest as I introduced him to the many and varied technical aspects of brushing and shovelling. The slow drag, the retreating shovel, the final flick – he was fascinated.

'It's all in the wrist,' I told him.

He nodded.

The drizzle had been sending out advance scouts to see how the land lay and now, acting on their reports, it began a mass offensive.

'So that's it then – I've got to go in now.'

The saturated fur on his head had separated, re-vealing a 1920s parting just above his left ear – he could have played opposite Clara Bow. His face was a picture of concentration – he had a big decision to make and I waited.

With one decisive shuffle and a wiggle of the hips, he forced his head between the roots and through the hedge, his ears pinging back and forth against the twigs.

His rear-end followed as a matter of course and then, taking a dozen tentative steps across the paving stones, he came over to me and sat on the shovel.

We looked at one another. We both had a decision to make – we both knew that whatever happened now, it was for life.

I smiled and he smiled and then I put down the brush, picked up the shovel, and carried him into the house.

Chapter Two

It takes time to break through the wall of Aileen's concentration. She sat at her desk, gazing at the screen of her word processor, but her mind was out there on the bleak moors of Yorkshire, observing the scene with a cool neutrality as her villain was savaged to death by a pig. She's a strange woman.

The letters she typed came up black and large – three inches high, five to the screen, before they moved off stage-left to allow others to take their place.

Her right eye gave up the ghost years ago and the left sees only light and shade and big blobs like letters three inches high. The retina in that eye is on its last legs and by rights she should see nothing at all. She's also a remarkable woman.

I coughed but she didn't notice. I felt a bit silly standing by her desk holding a shovel with a kitten on it. I coughed again and she came back into the real world.

'I've brought someone to see you.'

She looked up at my face for further explanation and then peered around my body towards the door.

'He's here – on the shovel.'

I lowered the kitten, JCB-like, until the two were face to face and then Aileen screwed up her eyes and moved in close.

The kitten swayed back, but held his ground as though his bum had been stapled to the shovel.

She stroked his head.

'Aren't you beautiful?'

He nodded in agreement.

'You're wet through.'

He stood up and shook himself and I had to steady him in case he fell off the shovel.

'Come on, let's dry you off.'

She carried him into the kitchen and I parked the shovel in the porch. By the time I joined them he had disappeared into the depths of a warm towel and was being rubbed dry by an expert who had practised on four small children.

He emerged looking as though he had been plugged into the mains. His eyes were wide and his fur fluffed out so that he was now a completely round kitten.

'There, that's better.'

He didn't seem so sure about that, and he padded along the draining board with the unsteady gait of a kitten who has just put on four and a half stone in weight.

'What's his name again?'

'Tigger.'

'He doesn't look like a Tigger.'

'He *looks* like a barrage balloon.'

My mother used to wash her cat in the sink and then blow-dry him until he was a foot across. The kitten wasn't in the same class as Whisky – but he could have been a contender.

He had another plate of chicken, just a little leg and a slice of wing this time – Aileen prepared it for him and she is known for her meanness, but he seemed to enjoy it, and after allowing him the luxury of a large drink and a small belch I carried him into the study and plonked him down on Aileen's desk.

'You ought to take him back now.'

'It's still raining and they're not home yet.'

'Soon then.'

He was fascinated by Aileen's gadgets. Strange instructions came up on the word processor screen as he minced across the keyboard on his way to the close circuit television – then on to the fax machine where he paused and lowered his bottom over the grill. A wave of pure pleasure passed across his face as the warm air rose and ruffled his tail-feathers. Then he sat down with a thump and grinned across at us.

'It's better than my bucket is this.'

I didn't want to take him back. It wasn't just that I felt sorry for him – there was more to it than that and I couldn't understand it.

I had never been a cat lover. I didn't dislike them – I stroked other people's and had always found kittens to be charming little creatures, but I had always imagined myself with a dog. A big dog – one that would come running at the sound of my voice and then sit gazing up at me adoringly.

Cats aren't like that. They are independent little devils with minds and lives of their own and they carve out careers for themselves with never a by-your-leave.

I glanced down at the kitten, who had now parked himself on my foot – he gazed up at me adoringly.

Aileen's voice drifted over from the desk.

'You're not thinking of keeping him, are you?'

'No – of course not.'

'I thought you always wanted a dog.'

I looked down at the kitten again and for one solid moment I thought he was going to bark.

'I should take him home now,' she said.

Aileen came over to sit with us and he seemed to realize that this was make or break time. He stood up – perhaps he was going to fetch my slippers – but no, his tiny mind was working overtime and then, warily skirting the very edge of the sheepskin rug as though it might bite him, he went over to the opposition.

He started on her ankles. Most cats are good with ankles but this kitten was something else – he worked with his whole body as though he had served his apprenticeship in a Bangkok massage parlour, he rubbed and nudged and eased and squeezed with back and flank and cheek and chin until Aileen bent double and hoisted him up on to her lap.

As she stroked him, his head pushed up to meet her palm, and all the while he purred like a diesel engine on a frosty morning.

It was a Pavarotti of a purr – deep and resonant, with just a touch of untutored roughness about it that took one back to the early days of the young Rod Stewart.

It even surprised the kitten and he stopped purring to listen to himself, but he couldn't hear anything so he kick-started his Tannoy system back into action and concentrated on the job in hand.

His paws shook and his fur rattled as he climbed and sat on her chest and then he went for the big one. I could almost hear him thinking.

'This always gets 'em.'

He fell on his side and with his head on her shoulder he played gently with the huge drop-earring that hung from her lobe like a punchbag, tapping it this way and that before standing up and bopping it with his forehead.

'Isn't he cute?'

He was sickening. Whose bloody kitten was it anyway? All right it was Patrick's, but with me it had been two blokes together, an understated, unspoken bond between two mates who weren't about to embarrass one another with a show of undue affection.

Now here he was, the chocolate box kid himself, playing Aileen as though she were a musical instrument – any moment now he would produce a box of Black Magic. I stood up.

'I think perhaps I should take him home now.'

She tickled him under the chin and his eyes closed and his legs buckled.

'There's no hurry,' she said, 'they'll hardly have missed him yet.'

The show went on for another half an hour or so and he was now hamming it up like an old actor-manager. I read the paper and pretended to ignore the pair of them. Aileen was completely under his spell. She would have cashed a cheque for him – he only had to ask.

Every time I snook a glance in their direction I

21

caught the kitten's eye and wished I hadn't and then he did the most remarkable thing.

He was walking across her breast-bone on his way to having a go with the other earring when he stopped, did a double take, and stared at her eyes – first one and then the other.

He'd stopped acting. This was the kitten I had picked up on the shovel. He turned and shuffled nearer to her face, placed his paws on her throat and rested his chin on hers.

For several minutes he took stock, scrutinizing her pupils like some small ophthalmic surgeon. Aileen sat very still and waited.

She has lovely eyes – you have to get up very close to see the black dots and scars of past operations. Sometimes a photograph will betray her – she can't see the lens and one eye will search for it whilst the other couldn't care less.

But unless they were told, or watched as she walked through a plate glass window, no one would ever know that she was blind.

But the kitten knew, and as we waited, he sat up and, placing one front paw on her cheek, he gently stroked her blind eye with the other.

We were spellbound. He touched his paw against the other eye and thought about it for a while, then keeled over and fell fast asleep on her shoulder.

'Did you see that?'

'Yes.'

'He could tell, couldn't he?'

'Yes.'

'Good God.'

*　　*　　*

At that point we had no idea that he had now taken up the vacant post of official guide-kitten, but he assumed his duties the moment Aileen peeled him from her shoulder and laid him down gently on the arm of the chair.

He awoke before she had taken a single stride across the room and then there he was, dancing in front of her like one of Vienna's Lippizaner horses, sideways and backwards, first his eyes on her feet and then on the doorway.

'*Clear the way please – clear the way.*'

Out in the hall he tried to steer her round the Chinese rug. He seemed to have a thing about rugs, they were black holes into which kittens disappeared, never to be seen again.

Aileen had no such hang-ups and she strode straight ahead, not seeing the frantic antics of the tiny ball of energy at her feet – and it was at that moment that his lack of formal training let him down.

'*Stop!*'

But Aileen didn't hear him. He hurled himself in front of her high heels without a single thought for his own safety, and then wished he hadn't been quite so impulsive as she trod on him, stumbled and fell.

I picked her up, dusted her off and checked for bruises – there weren't any.

'Are you all right?'

'Yes – I'm fine. Where's the kitten?'

I bent down and scraped from the rug all that remained of a now rather flat kitten and checked him for signs of life. He opened one eye.

23

'Where am I?'

'Don't worry, love – he'll be all right.'

'I think I'm the best judge of that.'

'He just needs an injection of chicken – straight in the vein.'

He lay limp in my palm and managed only the merest flicker of a smile.

'My hero,' he muttered weakly.

He managed to force down a morsel of chicken breast – well two saucers-full actually, but he made it quite clear to me that it was for medicinal purposes only and I shouldn't think for one moment that he was enjoying it.

He gave Aileen a wide berth as he wandered back into the hall. Chicken or no chicken – this being a guide-kitten wasn't going to be quite the picnic he had imagined.

Nevertheless he stuck to his task and raced ahead of her as she made for the stairs, then with a mighty leap he landed on the first step.

Without the long run-up it was going to take an even mightier leap to make the second and to his credit his chin made it, even if the rest of him didn't. He tried again, this time employing his own version of the Fosbury flop, but it's an old house with high ceilings and stairs to match and it was more than an uneven battle.

After another abortive attempt he graciously accepted a lift, and from the comfort of Aileen's arms he consoled himself with the thought that, from this elevated position, he could still be her eyes and ears and warn her if any vicious rugs were on the prowl.

I made myself useful and washed the pots. This was really Aileen's job – I did the cooking and she washed the pots, that was the unspoken agreement.

In reality I heated up the contents of various Marks & Spencer's boxes every day and she smashed several cups and a wineglass every night.

'What was that?'

'A gravy boat.'

'We haven't had any gravy.'

'I used it as a milk jug.'

She would travel around with her fingers in the bottom of the sink.

'What's that then?'

'That's the handle of the gravy boat.'

'What was wrong with the milk jug?'

'You broke it.'

We were fast running out of cups and saucers, plates and mugs. We were completely out of milk jugs and gravy boats and so I contrived to wash up as I went along, leaving just the odd pudding dish to tremble at her coming.

I rinsed out the milk bottles and went to stand them on the step. It was a pleasant night, the day had dried out and a full moon painted the balcony with soft light.

At times like this I have been known to have a stab at *Romeo and Juliet*. I only know four lines – if I'm down in the courtyard then it's Romeo who bursts forth in a pleasing baritone, delivered in an authentic, Cornetto-style, Italian accent.

'Buta soft! whata light through yonder window breaks?

It isa the east and Juliet isa the sun.'

Tonight I was up on the balcony and so it was in a Rank charm-school falsetto that I delivered the immortal lines,

'Good night, good night! parting is such sweet sorrow,

That I shall say good night, till it be morrow.'

Juliet is supposed to make her exit at that point, but an answering voice from down in the courtyard next door stopped me in my tracks.

'Is that you, Aileen?'

'No, it's me.'

Patrick sounded disappointed and I can't say I blame him. He shone a torch and caught me in its beam.

'Have you seen our cat? I can't find it anywhere.'

'No,' I heard myself saying, in a voice thick with innocence and sincerity. 'No – sorry, Patrick. I haven't seen it.'

Chapter Three

I followed Aileen around the bedroom as she tugged open first the wardrobe door and then the drawers in the dressing table.

'I can't believe you said that.'

Neither could I. I have been known to bend the truth a little. On occasions I have bent it until it snapped and there have been times when I stretched it until it winced, but I've never been a liar – just a bender and a stretcher now and then and it was mostly in a good cause.

'It just came out.'

She was lying flat on her stomach now, sweeping under the bed with her arm.

'You should have said you didn't know where he was.'

'Why?'

'Because I don't know where he is – I've lost him.'

I swept under the other side of the bed and then checked the shoe cupboard. I had to find him and take him home as soon as possible, then perhaps I might erase the bare-faced lie from my memory. I felt like a seven-year-old again.

'Honest, Daddy – I haven't seen the change you left on the mantelpiece.'

'What's that in your hand then?'

Would he believe that one of my insurance policies had matured? He didn't as a matter of fact, and the shame stayed with me long after the bruising had disappeared.

'Where did you see him last?'

'He was in the sink – eating the soap.'

'Right – let's do the bathroom again.'

We looked everywhere, I even went through the medicine cabinet. Aileen shook her head.

'He couldn't have got up there.'

'He got in the sink – how did he do that?'

'Jumped up off the toilet.'

I tipped the linen basket upside down for the second time that night, but Aileen didn't move.

'The lid on the toilet.'

'What about it?'

'It was up – I remember now, he tiptoed round the rim. He nearly fell in. He must have come down the same way.'

The lid wasn't up now, and we both stared at the closed toilet in horror.

'Have a look.'

I knew he would be in there. I could feel it in my bones and my bones are never wrong. I lifted the lid and he wasn't.

'No, he's not there.'

'Thank God for that,' she said and then added, 'he couldn't have gone down and round the bend, could he?'

'No – of course he couldn't.'

'You're sure?'

'Of course I am. Just don't flush it for a while.'

*　　*　　*

We couldn't find him anywhere. We combed the house from top to bottom and it's a big house. Eventually the clock in the hall struck twenty-three and a half minutes past one and we gave up and made for bed.

Aileen had one last look in the toilet – half expecting to see a tiny snorkel break through the surface of the water.

'I shan't be able to sleep – he could be suffocating.'

'Nonsense – he'll be all right.'

I wouldn't be sleeping either. I might as well do something.

'Where's my dressing-gown? I'll have one last look around.'

'I put it in the washing-machine, ready for the morning.'

She sat bolt upright in bed – I didn't sit bolt upright, I'm not as quick on the uptake as she is.

'We haven't looked in the washing-machine.'

I sat bolt upright – I catch on quick once I've been pointed in the right direction – and in no time at all I was in the utility room, yanking open the door of the washing-machine.

I couldn't see him at first – he was all wrapped up in my towelling robe. Then his head appeared from under a pair of pants and, so as not to waste too much energy, he opened just the one eye and glared at me.

'Do you mind? Some of us are trying to sleep.'

The clock in the hall struck forty-six and a half

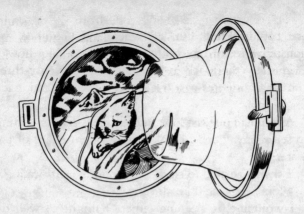

minutes to seven. I must do something about that clock – it's been in Aileen's family for just over a hundred years and it's time it went off on its own and saw what the real world is all about.

There was a pounding on my chest and a purring in my ear. I opened my eyes and a small white kitten was staring at me – if there's one thing I can't stand first thing in the morning it's a cheerful kitten.

'Go away.'

It moved up on to my throat.

'Ggggoooo aaawaay.'

It was fascinated by the throttling noise under its paws and began pounding like a washerwoman, my Adam's apple rolled gently sideways and plopped into my left ear. I picked him up and made to drop him down on to the bedside rug – he screamed.

'No, not that – anything but that.'

He broke free and scrambled back on the bed to tell Aileen all about it. I raced over and just managed to stop him in time – Aileen needs her eight hours.

Together we rescued my robe from the washing-machine and with my cigarettes and lighter in one pocket and a small white kitten in the other I padded downstairs to the kitchen.

'What do you fancy for breakfast?'

'*Chicken.*'

'There's none left.'

'*Prove it.*'

I opened the fridge door and we took stock. There was very little of anything in there and as he hung out of my pocket and examined the bottom shelf his face was a picture of misery.

I straightened and slowly raised him up a shelf.

'Second floor – butter, cheese, onion and herb dip, half a grapefruit.'

He sniffed and nodded. I straightened a little more.

'Third floor – half a tin of Fussell's condensed milk, one can of Coke and two salmon steaks.'

'*What's salmon?*'

'You wouldn't like that. Going up – fourth floor, six large eggs, bottle of french dressing, cranberry sauce, box of cherry tomatoes and . . .'

'*What's that?*'

'Garlic sausage.'

'*I'll try that.*'

He loved it, and by the time the kettle had boiled he had eaten two slices. I gave him a third slice, took my cup of tea into the study and spread the *Independent* out on the floor.

I can't read the newspaper sitting in a chair, I have to squat on all fours. It dates back to my early days with the *Beano* and the *Dandy* and causes all sorts of problems for me on the Inter-City trains to London.

The kitten put his head around the door and wanted to know where the hell was his milk. I apologized and followed his indignant little rump back into the kitchen – then slipped him a slice of Allinson's wholemeal bread under the grill.

We waited. It takes ages and then it's all done at once. You have to catch it while the smoke is still a bluey grey. I smiled down at him – he glared up at me.

'It won't be a minute.'

He glared up at me.

'It's wholemeal – it's good for you.'

He glared up at me and the penny dropped.

'You wanted milk, didn't you?'

He glared up at me.

'You didn't want toast.'

He glared up at me.

'I'm sorry.'

He glared up . . .

'Stop it!'

He rolled his eyes.

'And you can stop that as well. Who the hell do you think you are?'

The eyes widened in amazement.

'What'd I do?'

He didn't drink his milk right away – he waited for his toast. I felt rotten about being sharp with him and so I split it between us, marmalade on my half, Marmite on his and went back to the *Independent*.

He joined me a few minutes later and, with milk dripping from his chin, sat down on Nelson Mandela.

'I was reading that.'

He burped, and from the very depths of his soul a great wave of second-hand garlic sausage bubbled up and surrounded us. I went green and Nelson Mandela went white.

Even the kitten couldn't stand it. He tried to walk away from it, but the garlic followed him around the study like a low lying cloud and it took four high speed laps of the room before the cloud gave up and went off to take it out on the ozone layer.

He stretched out for a few moments on the window-sill and then came over and sat on Melvyn Bragg.

'Look – you are going to have to learn one or two ground rules. And the first one is this: in the mornings I like a little time on my own with the newspaper – got it?'

He nodded – he'd got it. He moved over and sat on the racing page.

I'm not at my best in the mornings. I have been known to clean my teeth with Savlon and I have sprayed under my arms with Elnett. I wasn't up to coping with a kitten who had bad breath.

I adapted the famous tablecloth technique where you yank a newspaper out from underneath a kitten without the aforementioned kitten knowing a damned thing about it – I yanked and he fell over, stuck his claws in the racing page and hung on.

I dragged him all the way out into the hall. He thought it was a wonderful game and he slashed out right and left at the bucking newspaper – bits were falling off all over the place as he shredded it to pieces.

I slipped my hand under his stomach and lifted him in the air for a nose-to-nose confrontation. The racing page came with him and he hovered in mid-air like an eagle with a rabbit.

'Right – that's it. I'm taking you home.'

'Can't you take a joke?'

'I should have done it last night – I can't think what I was playing at.'

He began purring and his undercarriage vibrated against my palm.

'And that won't get you anywhere either.'

He pushed his anxious little face closer to mine as he tried to work out just where he had gone wrong. I didn't mean to grin – it sort of escaped, but it was enough.

His face exploded and he smiled a smile that came up all the way from Cheshire. My heart melted and I leaned forward and touched his nose with mine.

Then he burped a burp that came up all the way from Hades – and the world began to spin.

Aileen curled up in the armchair, a cigarette in one hand, a cup of coffee in the other and, poking his head out of her dressing-gown, a small white kitten snuggled up against her naked breasts.

'There's nothing more sensuous than feeling warm fur against bare flesh,' she murmured.

So not content with waking me halfway through the night and shredding my newspaper first thing in the morning, this kitten was now taking over my role as a sex object.

'He reminds me of that cat in the Garfield cartoon – what's his name?'

'Garfield,' I told her.

'No – not him. The kitten, the cutest kitten in the world?'

'Nermal.'

'That's it – Nermal.'

She bent and kissed his head. He preened and, closing his eyes, pressed up for more attention. She kissed his nose – if he burped now she would discover that he was also the most toxic kitten in the world.

'We ought to take him home,' I said. 'I'll drop him off on the way out.'

Then I could apologize to Patrick, tell him that I had lied and beg his forgiveness.

Better still I could tell him that I had searched high and low for his kitten, rescuing it at the very last minute from the slavering jaws of a vicious Dobermann. That should have him round cutting my side of the hedge on Saturday afternoon.

'You're too late. They've gone out – I heard the gate click.'

'Damn.'

The kitten frowned – swearing again.

'Don't worry,' Aileen said, straightening out his ears, 'he'll be company for me. I'll take him round when Sarah comes home.'

Time was galloping on. I was due in Newcastle at twelve and I hadn't showered yet.

'I shall be late.'

I folded the newspaper as best I could and laid it

in strips on the table. To his credit the kitten looked embarrassed.

'Right then – I'm off upstairs.'

I walked slowly across the study, half hoping to hear the clatter of tiny hooves as a faithful kitten bounded after his beloved master. He slipped a couple of inches further down Aileen's cleavage, yawned and turned over on to his back.

'Me too,' said Aileen, 'I must get cracking.'

He was up like greased lightning, dancing across the carpet, ever watchful of her feet, and for one brief moment I thought he was going to open the door for her. He would have too, had he been able to reach the handle.

He waited for her in the hall like a small policeman on point duty, steered her efficiently round a disappointed Chinese rug and headed her off towards the staircase.

'Isn't he beautiful?'

'He's all right,' I agreed.

'He's lovely.'

'He's not bad.'

'He's very intelligent, you know.'

He sat on the bottom step and waited for a lift, as smug a kitten as ever sat on a bottom step and waited for a lift.

'Give him a hand, he can't manage it.'

For one brief moment I considered giving him a foot instead, but I am basically a kind man and so I scooped him up and placed him in a look-out position on Aileen's shoulder.

They took their time climbing the stairs and I moved ahead of them and turned towards the landing.

Behind me I heard Aileen break out into her Long John Silver impression, whilst the kitten sat bolted to her shoulder and pretended that he knew what a parrot was.

He laughed hollowly at her 'Ar, Jim lad's and rather nervously at her 'Shiver me timbers', but he must have felt very vulnerable up there as she affected the most outrageous limp.

Perhaps it was the relief of reaching the topmost step, for it was there that the kitten burped and the woman staggered and the kitten jumped and landed on the white sheepskin rug.

He knew then that his short career as a kitten was over – sheepskin rugs are the worst, most vicious kind of rug – and he froze and awaited his fate.

'What the hell's he been eating?'

'Shhh.'

He stood stock still for some time and then, as it began to dawn on him that this rug was probably one of the few friendly rugs in captivity, his fur relaxed and his ears went limp and his two front paws began to pound and pound and pound.

'What's he doing?'

'He's pounding.'

The description didn't do him justice. His back was in spasm, his head was bowed, in fact the whole of his tiny body was a monument to ecstasy. Even the rug seemed excited.

'What's he doing now?'

'Still pounding.'

I had a shower and Aileen had a shower and when we came out he was still at it. I bent to stroke him and I could hear his motor running.

'It's my mother,' he purred, *'it's my mother.'*

Chapter Four

I love talking in the North-East. Some audiences sit tight, as sealed individual units, their arms metaphorically folded across their chests.

'Go on then – entertain us.'

You have to work to win their approval. In the North-East they welcome you with open arms and will you to do well.

Their standards are just as high and their criticism just as valid, but they understand that the next hour is to be a two-way thing, and as you stand up and clear your throat they are already switched on and rooting for you.

You can still fail to last the course, but at least they give you a flying start.

The only thing that ever comes between me and the North-East is the A1. That's where you earn your money – not on the platform.

The road-works stretch for miles ahead. The salesmen in their Ford Sierras chew on the steering wheel, the vegetarian in the Citroën 2CV chews on his bar of nuts and raisins, and the man in the Reliant Robin contentedly chews on his cud – he always travels at this speed.

Seven miles in two and a half hours. A man jumps out and kicks savagely at a traffic cone – the other cones move in on him menacingly. He jumps back in, locks his door and winds up the window.

At any moment a wooden cart with wooden wheels will come rumbling down the central reservation to the accompanying cry of 'Bring out your dead.'

Road-works. I saw an actual workman once and thought I was going mad.

Aileen was hard at work when I arrived home, sparks flying from her keyboard. I kissed her on the head and waited patiently for her to work her way back to the present day.

Right now she would be out on a North Yorkshire farm in the mid-1940s, persuading her characters to do as they were told. Sometimes the more wilful ones disobeyed her, they were the ones who made the book come alive. So I sat and waited – I didn't want her to get the bends.

As she moved into a book she wound herself around her characters and they in turn would influence her. I would keep an eye on my back as she consorted with the evil half-brother who was savaged by the pig. Keeping company with the blunt Mr Renshaw would turn her into a woman of few words.

I looked over her shoulder and saw that Maddie and Max were sinking down half naked by the hearth, their bodies intertwined, his lips caressing hers . . .

I waited for her – she would be worth waiting for.

I made a pot of tea and took the tray into the study. There was no sign of the kitten – she must have taken it home.

'Hello . . .'

She was coming down from the farm now, wiping the mud off her wellies.

'. . . how long have you been here?'

'Long enough to make a pot of tea – there's a cup in front of you, don't knock it over.'

'Lovely – thanks. Have you seen the kitten?'

'No.'

'I've lost him again. He spent all morning on the sheepskin rug, but I haven't seen him for ages.'

'I thought you'd taken him home.'

'No – I can't find him.'

We had eighteen rooms. She would have had trouble finding a buffalo. A kitten, even a white one, would be impossible. Some guide-kitten he'd turned out to be.

'You could have shut him in somewhere – where have you been?'

'I haven't been anywhere, honest. I've been working in here all day.'

'You must have been to the toilet . . .'

'Well, yes.'

'. . . and into the kitchen.'

'Only to get a yoghurt out of the fridge.'

There was a pause. It wasn't a long pause, it was a short pause, about three-fifths of a second in duration and then Aileen said, 'I couldn't have, could I?'

She could have and she had. The kitten sat on that

41

glass shelf that covers the vegetable tray – astride a polythene pack of Danish bacon.

His prim little paws were buttoned up side by side, and his miserable excuse for a tail was neatly tucked in – just like his mother had taught him.

'Sit up and don't slouch.'

As the light came on his eyes slammed shut. His mouth opened wide, but whatever it was he intended to say remained frozen solid inside him.

I knelt down and picked him up, and the Danish bacon came up with him – his bum welded to the polythene.

'Is he all right?'

'I don't know – it's hard to tell.'

I ripped the polythene like a plaster from his fur. His eyes shot open – he would get me for that later.

'Here – give him to me.'

I handed him over and reached for the towel.

'Wrap him in this.'

She waved it away and tucked him inside her shirt.

'He needs body warmth.'

She closed her arms around him and cuddled him against her breast, but it was going to take more than that to melt him – he was a rigid little kitten, like a stuffed toy from Woolworths.

Aileen began to shiver.

'C-could he have frost-bite?'

'I've no idea.'

Her eyes frosted over and her teeth began to chatter, but the kitten just lay there like a pubescent snowball. He seemed to have shrunk.

'Pass me the towel and let's get him by the fire.'

She wrapped him up tight, and I had the fire on full blast by the time she plonked him down on the hearth in the drawing-room.

She held him in the glow of the fire and rubbed him gently with the towel.

'Don't hold him too close – he might get hot-aches.'

She rubbed his paws to make sure they weren't missed out as his blood began to circulate and gradually, here and there, certain bits of him came back to life and started to move.

First it was his head that nodded up and down, slowly as though he might be in the rear window of a Ford Cortina. Then his tail, such as it was, swished hesitantly like a short-sighted pipe-cleaner.

'I think he's going to be all right.'

He looked up at me and I could read his mind.

'We're a vet now, are we?'

And then he began to shiver. I have never seen anything shiver quite like that kitten. If Aileen had let go of him we would never have caught him again.

He moved through from first gear to fifth gear and then on to automatic – his whole body trembling, every little muscle pulsating and it seemed as though he was never going to stop.

'I've got an idea.'

With hindsight it was perhaps not the brightest idea I have ever had, but at the time I thought I was a genius.

'My thermal vest!'

I raced into the kitchen and pulled open the duster drawer. A couple of weeks earlier I had washed the vest and then stuck it in the tumble-dryer on hot.

When I pulled it out an hour later it would have fitted Action Man and it had been condemned to spend the rest of its working-life polishing horse brasses.

'Try and hold him still.'

I eased his head through the top and then tied the two short sleeves round the back of his neck in a bow. With a pair of scissors I made four small holes and pulled a leg through each.

'What do you think?'

'He looks ridiculous.'

'It's not finished yet – hold his tail up.'

I tied what remained of the vest in a huge ungainly knot so that a little skirt with a bump in it trailed down behind him.

'Well?'

'He'll probably never forgive you.'

I tidied up the loose slack with a couple of safety pins, a paperclip and the staple gun.

'There – it could have been made for him.'

'By whom exactly?'

At least he had stopped shivering. Either the thermalolactyl qualities of the vest were working their magic or it was shock induced by catching a glimpse of himself in the mirror – whatever it was his little motor gradually began to wind down and to celebrate I treated him to a saucer of lightly mulled milk.

Aileen put him down and he took a few tentative steps towards the saucer, a pool of thermal vest trailing behind him as he moved along the hearth rug.

'He looks like Dopey.'

'No he doesn't.'

'Could you make him a floppy hat?'

Sometimes I think the woman has no soul.

He slept for an hour or more. Aileen brought his mother, the sheepskin rug, down from the landing and after a luxurious pound and a good long stretch he curled himself up into a ball and slept like a kitten.

I must admit he did look slightly ridiculous and I wondered what would happen when he woke up and found himself encased in a thermal strait-jacket.

I needn't have worried – he loved it. He had a bit of a nibble at the safety pin that stretched the fabric tight across his manly chest and a quick furk at the bow on the back of his neck, but then he yawned and snuggled down into the rug once more.

He seemed to accept that this was something that happened to kittens when they reached a certain age.

We watched Clive James on television that night. Aileen can't see him, but the way he juggles with words makes for good radio and I do my best with the visual stuff.

'They're burying a Japanese up to his neck in the sand.'

'Who are?'

'Some other Japanese.'

'Why are the audience laughing?'

'I've no idea.'

The kitten sat between us and hung on my every word – Clive James was slightly above his head, but I work at a mental level which kittens find appealing and he seemed to appreciate my interpretation.

He had thawed out now and the warmth of his thermal-vested shank, pressed firmly up against my thigh, was comforting. I stroked him and he purred.

I had a puppy for my sixth birthday. A week later I came down early one morning and stroked him as he lay in his basket. His body was firm and solid, unresponsive and very dead. I hadn't wanted a pet since then – they die on you. Much better to throw a stick for a stranger's dog in the park, make a fuss of it and then walk away.

'They're letting lots of tiny crabs loose now.'

'What are they doing?'

'They're crawling all over their heads.'

The kitten shuddered and caught my eye.

'What's on the other channel?'

It was football and he seemed to like football. He jumped down and sat right in front of the television, his head sweeping through thirty degrees like the gun turret on a Sherman tank.

Lee Chapman belted the ball over the Coventry crossbar and the blessed John Motson looked deep into the recesses of the striker's mind and knew exactly what he was thinking.

'The veteran will be kicking himself for missing that one,' he claimed.

Veteran? What did he mean veteran? I played in the same team as Lee Chapman's dad in the Air Force.

The kitten turned his head and looked up at me.

'It bobbled as he hit it.'

On the television Trevor Brooking stepped in to defend the tall centre forward.

'I think you'll find, as we look at the replay, John, that it bobbled just as he hit it.'

The kitten nodded in agreement.

'Told you.'

Then he went off behind the television to see if he could find the ball.

'Where's Nermal gone?' asked Aileen, feeling the empty gap between us.

'He's gone to have a look for the ball – here he comes now.'

The kitten sauntered back round the video cabinet wearing his vest with all the panache of a Lagerfeld model.

'Can't find it.'

He sat down again to watch the match.

'Oh – they've got another one.'

'What about Thermal?' suggested Aileen.

'What about it?'

'For a name.'

'I like it.'

She leaned forward and spoke to the kitten.

'What about you Thermy? Do *you* like it?'

His tiny ears pricked in response but then Cyrille Regis was brought crashing down in the penalty area and the referee pointed dramatically to the spot.

'Yes – whatever. I'm busy at the moment.'

And in that brief moment we had formally adopted a small white kitten. Unethically – and probably illegally – but it was none the less binding for all that.

Not only did he now have a new name, but in the

mere thirty seconds or so since his christening it had shrunk with the warmth of affection.

I would pop round next door and have a word with Patrick in the morning – I had a lot of explaining to do.

Chapter Five

Thermal spent the night in Aileen's study. There are better ways of waking up in the morning than having a kitten jumping up and down on your face and so I decided to start off as I meant to go on.

He wasn't going to get spoilt for a start. I just made up a simple bed for him on the recliner chair – a travelling rug for a base, surrounded by three cushions so that he couldn't fall off and then I plumped it up and made it all nice and soft. He was going to have to learn to rough it.

Aileen had placed a saucer of water for him on her desk which was a very thoughtful touch and we each gave him a last pat on the head before we said good night.

'Do you think I should take his vest off?'

Aileen thought about it as I turned the chair away from the window so that the light wouldn't wake him too early in the morning.

'You realize he might not be house-trained?'

I hadn't thought about that.

'I'd better take his vest off then.'

'No, leave it on. Then at least, if he does anything, it will be all sort of – contained.'

I didn't want to think about that at all. Since I had brought him in on the shovel the kitten had put away half a pint of milk, a little chicken, a lot of garlic sausage and a tin of sardines.

So I did what I always do in situations like that – I put it out of my mind and went off to bed.

He was up and waiting for me the next morning – his head plunged deep into the saucer as he finished off the last of the water.

I walked around and had a look at the other end. Everything seemed to be in order. One of the paper-clips had come adrift giving him the loose and baggy look of a Turkish pasha, but that apart he was extremely well turned out and he had about him the clean-cut air of someone who has already jogged, showered and cleaned his teeth.

The sun was shining and we breakfasted on the desk by the window. Down in the courtyard three cats took advantage of the morning warmth.

One sprawled on the dustbin, another sprawled on top of the one sprawled on the dustbin and a third looked thoroughly miserable with himself because there was nowhere left for him to sprawl.

I drew back the curtain and held Thermal up so that he could see.

'There, that's what cats do.'

He wasn't the slightest bit interested. He was mildly surprised that they weren't wearing thermal vests, but that was all.

'Come on then – let's get this off.'

I tugged at the knotted sleeves round the back of his neck and he went berserk.

'What are you doing?'

'You don't need it any more.'

He didn't agree with me and hid behind the letter-rack.

'Come on.'

'Go away.'

It wasn't the best of hiding places. His ears peeked over the top of Aileen's VAT return and his tail strayed perilously close to the pencil sharpener. I grabbed him and he made a jump for it.

We were both partially successful. I had him by the scruff of the vest and he dangled in mid-air like the basket from a hot air balloon.

'Get off.'

'All right.'

'I'm warning you.'

'All right – keep your fur on.'

I lowered him gently and his legs were travelling at thirty miles an hour long before his feet touched the carpet and then he was off across the study and out into the hall.

I found him sitting under the telephone table, sulking with his back to me. The knotted sleeves had loosened now and they hung limply from his head, giving him the appearance of a rather forlorn and somewhat disenchanted rabbit.

'You're being very silly.'

'Push off.'

'What did you say?'

'Nothing.'

We broke off diplomatic relations at that point. I went into the kitchen for a second cup of coffee and another slice of toast. He sat under the telephone table and stared at the skirting-board.

I have always felt that skirting-board staring is an over-rated pastime and it wasn't long before he became bored with it and strolled into the kitchen to see what all the clattering and scraping was about.

He gave the fridge a wide berth as he came round the door – it was cold in there and the bacon went for you.

He was coming apart at the seams. His vest had now wrinkled down round his ankles like Nora Batty's stockings and even Compo would have thought twice before venturing forth in such an outfit.

I was on my knees, scraping butter off the carpet, and he came over to help me. We worked together in silence, me with a knife, him with his tongue. The two of us together had it cleaned up in no time.

'I'm sorry.'

'So am I.'

'I get carried away.'

'I should have asked first.'

It's always good to clear the air but that first quarrel takes the steam out of you and there was a distance between us that hadn't been there before.

The sultana helped to take his mind off things. He found it in front of the rubbish bin. It was hiding just under the pedal and it frightened him at first. It was big for a sultana and he had never seen one before.

He stalked it for a while – he'd practised stalking on the smaller leaves in the courtyard, but he would be the first one to admit that he had a lot to learn. The bigger leaves had taught him that.

The sultana was just as cautious – in all probability it would never have seen a kitten wearing a thermal vest before, but after a tentative poke and a quick run and a hide together behind the vegetable rack they got on famously and were soon charging all over the house.

It's easy to laugh at a kitten who falls in love with a sultana, but it was the very first thing he had ever owned and we all remember our first bike, don't we?

I sorted out my mail on Aileen's desk and carried it into my office. She keeps a tidy desk, just the essentials plus cigarettes, lighter and an ashtray.

I need clutter – files, books, dozens of pens, lucky horseshoe, a pair of pliers, birthday cards, a small white kitten in a thermal vest and a sultana.

They sat under the heat of the Anglepoise lamp and watched me work – it was the first time the sultana had been in here and Thermal showed him around.

'That's his phone.'
'Fascinating.'
'And that's his photocopier.'
'It's a different world, isn't it?'

The three of us worked together for a while. I answered my mail, Thermal sat in the wastepaper basket, shredding envelopes with a quiet efficiency, and the sultana stood shoulder to shoulder with a small brass paperclip, taking it all in and learning.

It was a scene that would be repeated all over the country, in office after office, at nine o'clock that morning. The older hand, the office boy and the junior, each contributing, in his own way, to the wealth of a great nation.

And then, in office after office, the boss would come in – disrupting the well-oiled operation with outrageous demands.

'Tea,' croaked Aileen as she passed through the hall, en route to her much larger office.

In the raw hours of the morning her speech-patterns resemble that of the early American Indian – short staccato words that leave no doubt in the mind as they stab into the subconscious.

Two teas and a black coffee later she would slowly evolve into the soft and gentle creature that we all knew and loved so well – first thing in the morning she was a cross between Joanna Lumley and Geronimo.

I made her a cup of tea and with Thermal riding shotgun, took it into her study – we left the sultana to look after the phone.

She had an envelope under the close circuit television and was peering at the screen with the aid of a magnifying glass.

'Where's that?'

I plucked it out from underneath the television and examined the postmark.

'Eastbourne.'

'Don't know anybody in Eastbourne.'

'Open it and find out.'

'What's that?'

'A window.'

She tossed it aside. 'Don't like windows – where's that one?'

'Kendal.'

'That must be Mollie.' She ripped open the envelope, thrust the letter under the television, and then with the magnifying glass she began to read slowly like a child, moving her lips silently as she worked her way down the screen.

What is it with postmarks? Without the close circuit television she can hardly see the envelope and yet she still feels the need to decipher a semi-smeared blob before venturing into the interior.

'Damn.' She gave up halfway and rubbed her eyes. 'I can't make it out.'

'I'll read it to you.'

'Let me have another try first – where's the saucer?'

'Saucer?'

'It was on my desk.'

'This one?' I pushed it towards her.

'That's it.'

Very carefully she traced the saucer with her finger and then stopped short.

'You've spilt it.'

'I haven't.'

'It had water in it.'

'Last night – yes.'

'You've spilt it.'

'No I haven't. Thermal drank it.'

The kitten was warming his bottom on the fax machine. His vest was having a nervous breakdown and he looked like a small rag and bone man.

'He what?'

'You left it out for him and he drank it.'

'I was soaking my contact lens – I couldn't find my case so I left it in the saucer overnight.'

I glanced across at Thermal. He was just leaving his post and as he walked across the machine his paws dialled 071 for Inner London. Aileen heard the tones and turned to face him.

'Thermal?'

'He must have swallowed it.'

'He can't have.'

I took the saucer over to the window but there was no sign of the contact lens.

'When he drinks his milk it flies all over the place.'

We searched the desk inch by inch and then went down on all fours and combed the carpet. The kitten peered over the edge of the desk to see what we were up to. Aileen had an idea.

'You remember last time I lost it – you found it stuck on my cheek.'

We both reared up to examine the kitten at close quarters. First a general once-over and then we zoomed in really close for a more detailed inspection. The kitten backed off.

'*What?*'

'It's all right – don't worry.'

'*I shall tell my dad.*'

'We won't hurt you.'

'*Better not.*'

I frisked his whiskers and raked the fur on the top of his head and cheeks with my finger nails –

that's all I could get at, the remainder of his sturdy little body was encased in the now fashionably-loose thermal cotton.

'It could have slipped inside his vest,' Aileen suggested, and for once in my life I took a major policy decision without resorting to arbitration, breast beating or a long lie down. With one almighty yank I had a thermal vest in one hand and a rather surprised kitten in the other.

As we shook out the vest he sat on the desk wearing nothing but a huff and never once did he take his eyes off me.

'I never thought you would sink to such depths.'

'I'm sorry – but it had to be done.'

'You wait.'

We searched all over the place but the contact lens was nowhere to be found.

'At least it's insured,' Aileen comforted herself.

'I suppose technically it's not even lost. We know where it is. We could even get it back again.'

'I don't think I shall fancy it then.'

I made some toast for Aileen and another pot of tea for both of us and poured the merest dribble in a saucer for Thermal – just to watch him in action. He grimaced.

'Not enough sugar.'

I obliged and he tried again.

'Spot more milk?'

By trial and error I got it just about right and he drank the lot. We watched closely to see how far the splashes went but it didn't really help us any and so we closed the file on the case of the missing contact lens.

The little kitten jumped up on to the bookcase above the desk and then began to tightrope-walk as the books became thicker and more substantial and the ledge became narrower.

'Be careful – you'll fall.'

'Don't worry about him,' said Aileen. 'He's got eyes in his backside.'

I couldn't have put it better myself.

Chapter Six

There was a notice scrawled on the pet shop window. 'Closing Down – Everything must go.' Everything had almost gone and the shop echoed emptily like a newly decorated room before the curtains are hung and the carpet laid.

Tatty paper sacks spilled dog biscuits down on to the bare boards and in a cage by the window sat the scruffiest looking budgie I'd ever laid eyes on. He was a sort of yellowy-beige colour and he hadn't seen a comb in years.

He was the kind of budgie who ought to have had a fag hanging out of the corner of his beak and one wing stuffed deep down inside his pocket as he leaned against his mirror, making rude gestures at the passing pigeons. Sellotaped to his cage was the sign, 'Shop-soiled – Half price.'

I wanted to take him home with me, but Aileen said he probably drank meths or took drugs or something and would be a lot more trouble than he was worth.

There was a tortoise in a glass tank with 'Ten per cent off' stuck on its shell, and since its head seemed to be missing I assumed that was the 10 per cent they were talking about. However, the owner assured me that it did actually have a head – it was hibernating.

'Anyway,' he said, 'it was only a joke.'

The puppies were segregated into two distinct lots. A couple of posh ones lolled in a pen by the fishtank and looked suitably bored with life, whilst on the other side of the shop a small herd of runts dashed around and collided with each other under a large sign which read, 'Reduced.'

I wanted to take four puppies as well as the shop-soiled budgie but Aileen talked me out of it once more.

'We came in for a cat litter-tray.'

They didn't have one and so we popped round the corner to see the opposition who were driving them out of business.

They had a dozen different litter-trays ranging from a rather basic mini-skip right up to the deluxe model suitable for hauling heavy freight on the Manchester Ship Canal.

'That's the one.'

'It's enormous.'

'He might want to have his friends round every now and then.'

'He won't be cleaning it out – you will.'

'That's true.'

The shopkeeper came over to help. I couldn't see the one I really wanted.

'Maureen Lipman has one with a roof.'

'Does she now?'

'Her cat does.'

'Well she won't have bought it here then.'

'No – she lives in London.'

'Ah well, she'll have bought it down there then.'

'Yes, I suppose she will have.'

As conversations go, it sort of went all limp and not where I wanted it to go at all.

'Which one would you suggest?'

'That one.'

That one was the Kitty Corner Cat Pan complete with its own Litter Enclosure and priced at £8.61. It was finished in a pleasing brown and cream and looked just the thing for today's modern cat.

For £1.99 we bought a large bag of Thomas Cat Litter with added Super Blue Deodorant Granules and then lashed out on a dozen tins of Whiskas Supermeat and a box of Brekkies – *prepared with real pilchard*. I had no idea there was so much to owning a cat – if Patrick wanted it back now he was going to have to take out a mortgage.

I hoped Thermal would be pleased – the litter-tray wasn't as spacious as some of those we had seen, but at least there was sufficient room in there for a cosy candle-lit dinner for two and drinks afterwards in the alcove. I thought that was much more romantic.

He loved it, and spent the whole afternoon curled up in one corner, fast asleep.

'He likes it, doesn't he?'

'He's not supposed to sleep in it,' Aileen pointed out. 'It's for crapping in.'

'I can't seem to get that through to him.'

'Show him.'

'Perhaps later.'

It became the focal point in Thermal's life – his leisure centre and his health farm. One day, when he was grown-up, he would establish this haven as a meeting place for great minds.

He entertained his little friend the sultana in there one morning and then panicked when he lost him amongst the granules. I had to sift and shake until the wizened little grape finally burst spluttering to the surface.

The kitten sat to attention in the far corner of his tray and watched me cook for the three of us – a Marks & Spencer's prawn and cod pie for Aileen and myself, a succulent coley steak for Thermal.

'There you are. Be careful, it's still hot.'

'I'll have it in here.'

'Oh no you won't.'

'Why not?'

'You'll have it out here – that's for peeing in.'

His look was incredulous.

'You're joking?'

'I'm not.'

He looked around him at the gleaming plastic and gently stroked the sparkling blue and grey granules with his paw – the granules he had raked smooth until they had taken on the aesthetic simplicity of a Japanese garden.

He looked up at me once more, examining my face. And then the worried frown softened with relief into a sunny smile.

That Deric – he's always pulling my leg.

I couldn't understand how he was holding it all in. His little stomach couldn't be any bigger than a tennis ball and yet he was a trencherman of the highest order. Maybe he was constipated – they had pills in the pet shop, I would have a word with them.

After dinner I went back to work. I can't think sitting at a desk, I do my best work lying on my back on the floor, and so I went into the drawing-room and lay down on the carpet by the radiator.

Thermal came with me. If he was going to be a writer himself he'd better see how it was done. He lay down beside me and thought hard for thirty seconds or so until he fell fast asleep – this being a writer seemed a very pleasant occupation.

I turned over a radio piece in my head. It was to be about the spiders who drift into the house during late autumn when the weather turns nasty. I don't think it has anything to do with it being cold outside – it's simply that the television programmes improve around that time and then of course there's the bonus of live football on a Sunday.

Thoughts flew across my mind – passing the one travelling in the opposite direction, the thought that is always there: that this was no way for a grown man to earn a living.

I stared up at the leaves of an enormous Swiss Cheese plant. Aileen had polished the leaves that very morning and I was just thinking that she had missed the underneath bit when a small white kitten walked across my chest on its way to the plant pot.

I examined his undercarriage very closely as he padded over my face and then the leaves shook as he landed on the soft earth. He swung round slowly

like a polar bear on a glacier mint and then, lowering
his rear end down to a workmanlike height, he threw
his head back, closed his eyes and began to thrutch.

'No!'

He didn't seem to hear me.

'Don't you dare.'

I was scrambling to my feet and waving my arms.
The kitten's eyes were wide open now and his body
froze in mid-thrutch.

'What?'

'Don't you dare.'

'How do you mean?'

I plucked him off the plant pot and, holding
him out to dry in front of me, rushed him into the
kitchen.

'What are you doing? Put me down.'

I put him down in his litter-tray and then, sinking
back on my haunches, I waited. He was horrified. His
little face darted through a dozen different patterns as
he fought to regain control of his bowels. Finally his
expression came to rest at smug and he relaxed a little.

'Come on.'

'No.'

'Do it here.'

'Here?'

'Yes.'

'Never.'

'Right.'

I picked him up again and, racing out through the
back door, carried him down the steps and into the
courtyard. A thin drizzle danced halfheartedly on
the rhubarb leaves as I planted his bottom firmly on the

wet soil. He shuddered in disgust but he could see that he was now dealing with a hard man who wasn't prepared to discuss the matter any further.

'Don't look then.'

That seemed reasonable enough. I turned away and walked back up the steps. From the balcony I had a bird's-eye view of a small kitten who had held on far too long and was now having a hell of a job persuading his bowels that he hadn't meant it and for God's sake stop sulking.

His little body flexed itself like that of a weight-lifter going for the big one. The shoulders swooped, the neck braced itself, the brain locked into neutral and the back protested violently. The head looked towards the heavens for help and then he saw me watching him – I turned away.

When I looked down again he was covering up the evidence – shifting great lumps of sodden soil that rolled on and then immediately rolled off again. It would have been a damn sight easier than this in the comfort of his own plant pot.

The huge wooden gate to next door's courtyard swung open and Patrick appeared.

'Hello there.'

'Hi Patrick.' Oh God – he'll see Thermal.

He came over to his side of the hedge for a few words while here on my side the little kitten heard the footsteps approaching and peeked at our neighbour's feet through the roots. From up on the balcony I felt like an umpire at some weird sort of tennis match.

'You look as though you've had a hard day, Patrick?'

'I recognize those boots.'
'They're all hard, Deric . . .'
'That voice rings a bell.'
'. . . wish I was a writer – sitting in the warm all day.'
'From a long time ago – back in my past.' The kitten rearranged his head to get a better-angled look.
'There's my bucket – it's all coming back to me now.'
He tried to work his way through the roots – his childhood had been spent on that bucket – but the roots were too thick for him and he got his shoulders stuck.

'That kitten hasn't come back.'

'It hasn't?' It was doing its level best right at that very moment. In no time at all it would have the hedge over.

'There's something I ought to tell you, Patrick,' I started, but mercifully the wind blew my words away and he didn't hear me.

'Anyway,' he went on, 'it's probably for the best. I'll bet it's found a good home, and it was no life for it here – not with us out all of the day.'

The kitten who had found a good home was now backing out of the leafy cul-de-sac and making his way down to the gap in the hedge when he disturbed a moth who should have been dead weeks ago.

God had kept it alive just for this very moment. As moths go it was knackered, but it had just enough staying power to keep it inches ahead of Thermal as it led him a dance across the courtyard and well away from the hedge.

'Anyway – must get some work done before the light goes.'

Patrick began to haul stones across to the small wall he was building and over on my side of the hedge the kitten was putting on a ballet worthy of an Arts Council grant.

It had been a long hard summer for the moth and, try as it might, it couldn't raise itself up over a foot above the ground, but since the kitten had a high jump record of only nine and a half inches there wasn't going to be an awful lot of blood spilt on the courtyard.

Then the moth made a bad mistake. It dropped dead in mid-air and Thermal caught it. He had never counted on this happening and he panicked. He stirred its inert body once with his paw and told the moth that he was only joking, but then, when it didn't move, he turned straight round and made for the gap in the hedge.

Then I panicked. I couldn't shout at him or Patrick would hear me and we weren't ready for that yet – and so I coughed. The kitten stopped and I coughed again. He looked up.

'What?'

'Humph!'

'Now – this minute?'

'Humph!'

'Oh – all right then.'

He took a slight detour to avoid the corpse and padded back up the steps.

'That's a bad cough you've got there,' shouted Patrick.

'Pleurisy,' I shouted back.

'What is?' asked the kitten as it reached the balcony.

'Humph!' I told him as I helped him in through the door with my foot.

'All right,' he grumbled as he pitched headfirst across the hall carpet, *'keep your hair on.'*

Chapter Seven

From that moment on Thermal developed a deep love of the great outdoors. At eight o'clock the following morning he was sitting on the doormat waiting to be let loose once more.

'Not on your own. You're not old enough yet.'

'I'm not on my own.'

He had his sultana with him but that wasn't going to sway me – we cat owners have to be firm at times.

'You can sit there all day if you like, but it won't make any difference.'

As it happens he didn't sit there all day – the postman almost killed him.

He shoved a couple of bills and a selection of catalogues from Hartington House, Scotcade and Kaleidoscope through the letterbox. These puny items merely bruised Thermal's ego.

It was the Yellow Pages that did the real damage.

One minute I was being firm with a healthy young cat, the next I was sweeping up into my arms the victim of a vicious hit-and-run attack and also giving the kiss of life to his friend – a sultana with brain damage.

I carried the pair of them into the drawing-room and laid them down by the radiator. Of the two, the sultana made the least fuss – Thermal never stopped whimpering.

First it was his leg and then it was his back. From what I could make out, he wasn't long for this world – he was sure of that.

He wanted me to have his litter-tray when he was gone. He knew I would treasure it and it was mine on the understanding that I would look after his unmarried sister in Brighouse.

Aileen was to have custody of the sultana for as long as it lived at home.

RADA would have snapped him up after a performance like that. I left him to it and went to help Aileen work her way through the catalogues. She sucked delicately on a small round mint.

'What's that?'

I read the small print.

'It's a vacuum-cleaner organizer.'

'What's it say about it?'

'It costs £6.99 and it's a plastic thing you stick on the wall to hold all your vacuum-cleaner attachments.'

'We've got one, haven't we?'

'Yes – ours is called a cup-hook.'

The selection was astonishing. There was *the handbag that grows on you*.

'That would frighten the life out of me.'

And a set of cast-iron kitchen scales. *The scales that weighed in Mrs Beeton's time will weigh as accurately today*.

'And take as much lugging about – what else is there?'

'How about *The handy, hungry fluff remover for well-groomed sweaters*?'

'What is it?'

It was an electric shaver, that's what it was. It's come to something when we go around shaving our sweaters.

The weirdest item of all was the *ceiling display clock*. It was advertised as the cleverest clock in the business. *You can tell the time – even in the dark.*

I could do that already – my bedside clock has a luminous display – but the single aim of these catalogues is to prevent you from having to do anything that looks like work, such as moving your head slightly to the right. All you had to do was to clap your hands and the sound-activated light display would beam the time up on to your bedroom ceiling.

I could tell the time without the ceiling clock. All I would have to do is clap my hands and there would be Aileen shouting, 'What the hell do you think you're doing at six o'clock in the morning?'

But she wasn't shouting now – she was choking. The mint had gone down the wrong hole and I patted her on the back.

'Humph! Humph!'

A small white flash arrived in the study doorway.

'What?'

'Humph!'

'I'm here.'

'Humph!'

Aileen collapsed across her desk, arms flailing, lungs screaming. I thumped again and a sticky white mint flew straight out and into her in-tray.

'Humph! Humph!'

'Don't cry.'

71

'Humph!'

'I'm here – tell her.'

He raced over and began to massage her ankles. She wiped her eyes and then picked him up.

'I'm all right now – he was worried wasn't he?'

'He thinks it's his name.'

'He thinks what is his name?'

'Humph.'

He waved my humph away in disdain.

'Do you mind – I'm talking to this lady.'

He told her all about his leg and all about his back and then, having got it out of his system, went and sat on the window-sill. I explained to Aileen all about Patrick and the coughing.

'So he'll come to me – every time I cough?'

'Try him.'

We went out to the hall and she coughed, gently into her hand.

'Louder.'

She raised the volume a little – nothing.

'He can't hear you.'

She coughed like a navvy on Capstan Full-Strength but it had no effect whatsoever. We waited for a minute or two and then poked our heads around the study door. He was squatting on the large plant pot in the corner, his eyes bulging, his nerve-ends straining, his back bent almost double like a bow.

'I'll be with you in a moment.'

We checked every plant pot in the house that night, some thirty in total, and he had been very thorough.

He was liberal with his favours – he had distributed a series of small torpedoes which were now in varying states of decay. He even pointed out a small bush I had missed in the bathroom.

'And here's one I prepared earlier.'

From then on I followed him everywhere he went. I had seen how it was done on the television and I was sure he had no idea he was being followed.

Just before midnight my heart leapt as he strolled into the kitchen and I watched through the crack in the door as he jumped into his tray and began to rake his granules. Was this the breakthrough I had hoped for?

No it wasn't. He wiggled his bottom a couple of times and then, sighing contentedly, he curled up into a ball and trained one eye on the crack in the door.

'Good night.'

I was going to have to be tough with this kitten – show him who was the boss. If he insisted on sleeping in his litter-tray then I was going to have to be ruthless.

I would start with a forced route-march down to the rhubarb patch – it was midnight, he could stay there until I was satisfied.

That would show him.

I stormed into the kitchen and he smiled at me. He looked so comfortable. I smiled back.

'Lights – if you don't mind.'

'Sorry.'

'It's all right – we all make mistakes.'

73

I could always start being ruthless in the morning.

That night in bed I mapped out a kitten-crushing routine of bread and water, cold showers and early rising – but I overslept and then had to abandon the idea altogether when Nick flew in from Dubai and the day was declared a public holiday in our house.

Thermal gave my son a somewhat subdued welcome. At first I thought this might be because his presence only served to highlight the fact that Thermal himself was adopted and not my natural heir, but it soon became clear that the kitten was wary of those enormous feet and was waiting to see if this one was blind as well.

Nick was amused by my relationship with Thermal and he spelt it out in the kitchen as we made a pot of tea.

'You know – you spoil that cat.'

'I don't.'

'You do.'

Nothing could have been further from the truth and I would have argued with him there and then but Thermal was about to jump off the kitchen table and it can hurt your paws can't it – jumping off the kitchen table?

So I picked him up and placed him gently on the lino tiles before smearing a thumb-full of Marmite on his saucer.

'What's that?'

'Marmite.'

'I don't believe this.'

'It's his elevenses – now if you'll excuse me.'

* * *

Thermal and I were developing a routine. The Marmite meant he had plenty of iron and it didn't lie heavy on his stomach as we went through our punishing schedule for the day.

I washed the pots as he pushed his saucer around the kitchen floor and then we went across to the office. He waited outside as I rolled a sheet of paper into a tube and then pushed it under the door.

Thermal on the other side saw it coming and went berserk. I wiggled it about and he chewed it and bit it and thumped it until it was dead and then we went off together to bank up the fire.

Nick had never seen me with a pet before and I tried to explain the relationship between a man and his cat.

'It isn't just a matter of letting it out at night and then chucking half a tin of Whiskas in a bowl when it comes back.'

'I can see that.'

'We're on the same wavelength – like the sheepdog and the shepherd on *One Man and His Dog* – we are one man and his cat.'

'In other words he's got you where he wants you.'

'Something like that.'

Thermal sat on the hearth and watched as I poked the fire – his was merely a passive role until the moment I took the lid from the coke bucket. Then his expertise came into play.

I picked out the coke with a pair of tongs and it was his job to sniff at each and every lump before

I placed it in position on the fire – a sort of quality control if you like. He had yet to reject a lump, but it was best to be on the safe side.

When that was done I was allowed to have five minutes with the paper whilst Thermal sat on the dining-room table and made faces at people passing by – I suppose it's more or less what everyone does with their cat in the morning.

To Nick this domestic scene of a man and his cat as one, in perfect harmony, was something new – something he had never experienced.

He was puzzled when I pulled out the middle pages of the paper and laid them beside me on the floor. He picked them up and handed them back to me.

'No, it's all right,' I told him. 'Thermal likes to sit on the paper when he's finished pulling faces at people. If I don't do that he sits on the bit I'm reading.'

'Why don't you just clip him round the earhole and tell him not to?'

But that was just the point. I'm bigger than Thermal and if I wanted to I could beat the living daylights out of him – but then if I did, would he sit on my chest all the way through *Coronation Street* with a paw each side of my neck and his head tucked under my chin?

Would he take just one bite of every meal I put down for him and then come looking for me to tell me that this was the best bit of fish he'd had in months before he went back and finished it off?

Would he sit on my desk all afternoon, sunning himself under the Anglepoise lamp, so that I could lean my notes up against him?

No of course he wouldn't, but Nick didn't seem to

understand and I was disappointed because you want those you love to love one another.

I spent the rest of the day working at my desk while Nick slept off his jet-lag on the settee. Thermal sat to attention on the sideboard to make sure he didn't run off with the silver.

An hour later I took a break and popped in to see if all was well and found that the kitten had taken his courage in both paws and was sitting in the armchair from where he could keep an eye on the cushions as well.

I made a cup of tea for Aileen and myself around six o'clock and on my way back to the office went to see if Nick was awake.

He was still flat on his back and out to the wide. His chest was rising and falling with each gentle, fluted snore and on his stomach was a small white kitten, riding it like a surfer rides a wave.

His concentration was absolute, but he looked up when he heard me come in.

'He's not much fun, is he?'

I watched *Coronation Street* with Aileen. She didn't sit with her paws either side of my neck or tuck her head under my chin – but apart from that she was quite good company.

Then I poured some wine and took the joint out of the oven. Aileen drank my wine, apologized and then drank her own.

'Better wake Nick.'

I pushed the door open slowly so that I could

bring him round in stages, but he was already awake and sitting by the hearth with Thermal.

They were trying to save the fire from extinction and Nick was plucking lumps of coke from the bucket with the tongs. He held out each and every lump so that Thermal could have a good sniff before he placed them in position on the grate.

With Nick's enthusiasm and Thermal's experience they made quite a good job of it and then my son unfolded the *Independent* on the carpet and began to read the television listings.

Thermal frowned, shifted impatiently and cleared his throat. Nick looked up.

'I'm sorry – I didn't think.'

He patted the little kitten on the head, plucked out the middle pages and spread them down by his side.

'There you are, old son – park your bum on that.'

That night we opened a bottle and talked into the early hours. It was well past Thermal's bedtime and he slept on Aileen's chest which, he had discovered – unlike Nick's chest or mine – had a special inbuilt design-feature that prevented him from sliding down.

He woke up as we were nodding off and looked longingly at the nearest plant pot.

'Oh no you don't.'

I picked him up and carried him down to the rhubarb patch. The cold air didn't seem to hit me until I reached the bottom step – there was a coating of white frost over the courtyard and I apologized as I put him down under a leaf.

'Sorry about this.'

'I should think so.'

He gave me one of his looks and so I left him
to it and spent the next minute or so persuading an
enormous black tom-cat that this wasn't a public right
of way. Thermal must have finished by now.

'You should have seen that one, Thermal – he'd
have made ten of you.'

There was no answer.

'It's all right – he's gone now.'

I couldn't see him anywhere. There was a full
moon and he was a white kitten – he'd almost glowed
when I had brought him down the steps.

'Thermal?'

Where was he? He hadn't come past me. I combed
the rhubarb patch and the full length of the hedge –
there was no sign of him. I remembered the cough.

'Humph!'

I coughed my way all around the courtyard and
back to the gap in the hedge. He must have gone
through to Patrick's – he'd be sitting on his bucket.
There was no other way he could have got out.

I'd have to go round – through the gate and down
the lane and then into Patrick's, hoping he hadn't got
it locked from the inside.

I fumbled my way across to the gate. It was a
heavy black gate in a shadowy stone wall and it was
wide open. We never left it open – must have been
the paperboy with the evening *Examiner*.

'Thermal. Come on, Thermal – there's a good
boy.'

It seemed darker out in the lane somehow, the

light from the windows didn't reach this far.

He could be anywhere and I had a funny feeling I was never going to see him again.

Chapter Eight

I sat on the wall of the West Indian Club and tried to imagine what the world would look like if I were only six inches tall. Where would I go if I were six inches tall?

Nick, who is six feet two inches tall, climbed the narrow steps from the park up to the dimly-lit lane and shook his head.

'It's no good.'

We had searched for two hours now and unearthed a regular army of cats. Some were off-duty – fast asleep in tumbledown outbuildings – and they had panicked at the sound of us and then looked guilty at being caught catnapping.

Others were wide awake and on guard. They spat at us, firing their rubber bullets indiscriminately. I was glad I wasn't six inches tall.

'We shan't find him tonight – not now.'

He was right. We walked back towards the house, sending the beam of our torches off into dark corners, pushing open gates with a nudge of the shoulder, listening to the intermittent roar of traffic on the main road not fifty yards away.

We had looked there first – in the gutter. You always look in the gutter. Cats seem to spin off when they have been hit by a car – they are very tidy animals.

We found three white paper bags that could have been him from a distance and a McDonald's polystyrene burger-box that definitely was him from only a couple of feet away.

'He'll be back in the morning – you'll see.'

Aileen stood on the balcony and whistled. She had the sort of whistle that would make the hair on a pebble stand to attention. Cats from the outlying villages put their paws over their ears and composed letters of complaint to the evening paper. The locals called in to complain in person.

They scattered as Nick and I pushed open our final gate for the night. Aileen hadn't seen them arrive and she didn't see them leave. For most of the time she treated her blindness as though it were no more than a slight cold, but at times like this she resented the fact that she had to be left behind like a child – to wait for the grown-ups.

The very first thing next morning I crept downstairs so as not to wake the others. I pushed open the door to the inner hall and padded down the corridor. I could almost see Thermal sitting on the step outside.

'He's not there – I've looked,' Nick shouted from the kitchen. I had a look anyway, just to make sure.

'He's probably sleeping it off somewhere,' he comforted as he filled the kettle, 'he'll be back before long.'

We heard Aileen feel her way downstairs, open the inner door and pad along the narrow hallway.

'He's not there – I've looked,' I shouted. But she had a look anyway – just to make sure.

*　　*　　*

The night before, draped in darkness, the lane had assumed an air of menace, as though it were auditioning for a Gothic novel. In the daylight you could see that it wasn't up to the job. Don't ring us – we'll ring you.

As a team we searched the gardens and outbuildings. Each of the old stone houses sprouted at least a shed or a garage apiece and some had an outside lavatory thrown in for good measure.

Nick and I peered in through windows and guiltily tried the locked doors. Some didn't have locks – some didn't have doors. Aileen whistled and coughed in turn and lifted the lids from dustbins but there was no sign of Thermal and we trooped back to the house a beaten bunch.

Earlier we had combed the park, like grouse-beaters spread out in an ineffectual line. We found an old man sleeping it off in a flowerbed, but he hadn't seen a kitten.

Before that I had climbed over the wall into Patrick's. I was feeling very guilty about taking his cat away from him – if I had left well alone then Thermal might still be here and better equipped to cope with life in the jungle. I had spoiled him rotten.

Nick had to leave that afternoon. It was Sunday and he was due down in Newport Pagnell for the start of a four-week course. We would have him for three more weekends before he flew back to Dubai.

After we had seen him off I sat down and put together an advert for the lost and found column in the *Examiner*. I offered a small reward for Thermal's return and if you are ever lonely and anxious to meet people I suggest you do the same.

The small boy held a bright ginger kitten in his arms. Either he had spent weeks training it to look pathetic or it just had a natural gift for being miserable.

'Is this it?'

'No, I'm sorry – mine was white.'

'This one's got some white on him.'

'Where?'

He turned the kitten over and examined its under-carriage.

'I saw some somewhere.'

'It's not mine, I'm afraid.'

'Why don't you buy it anyway. I can give you a choice – I've got three more at home.'

The girl was a little older and she needed to be if she was to hang on to the cantankerous tabby she held in her arms. It was at the very least ten years old.

'Are you the one who's lost a kitten?'

'Yes.'

'Is this it?'

'No – that's Ranji. He's Mr Patel's cat. Where did you find him?'

'In that garden on the corner.'

'That's Mr Patel's garden.'

'I'd better put him back then.'

'I think you had.'

The phone never stopped ringing and we made

a trip up to Lindley to look at a likely prospect.

'I'm sorry – it's not ours.'

'Thank God for that – I can keep it now without worrying.'

Other calls we could have done without.

'There's men going round stealing them you know. They make fur coats out of them and gloves and things – I wouldn't be at all surprised if he hadn't been taken. They have a van and they just chuck 'em in the back. My son says . . .'

I switched my brain off at that point – I didn't want to know what her son said.

Aileen rang the RSPCA, the PDSA and all the local vets and drew a blank each time. He couldn't have just vanished off the face of the earth, and my biggest fear was that he was locked in a building somewhere very close. He could have heard us calling him. I would rather have found him dead in the gutter than have him starve to death.

I kept telling myself that it was only a cat, but nothing is *only* anything and it was *my* cat and, as such, unlike any other cat in the world.

On the Wednesday morning I wrote a circular and wished I had thought of it earlier.

Have you accidentally locked a small white kitten in your garage or outhouse? He disappeared on Saturday night and hasn't been seen since. Would you please check.

I added my address and telephone number and ran off a hundred and fifty copies. By lunch-time I had pushed a hundred and thirty-two of them through letterboxes, some of which I never knew existed. And then I waited – I couldn't think of anything else to do.

The response wasn't overwhelming, but then we only needed one reply. We had two – one in person, the other via the phone.

The person was in his early twenties and he carried a half-starved cat under his arm. It was black and moth-eaten, with eyes so dull they seemed to have gone out.

'I don't suppose this is yours.'

'No – I'm afraid not.'

'I couldn't remember what you said yours was, I lost your note. Good job I checked though – it must have been in my shed a week. I've given it a feed.'

He put the cat down and suddenly it came to life. From the balcony we watched it race across the courtyard and out through the gate. It turned off the lane and on towards the main road – looking left and right before shooting straight across and up a garden path. The young man smiled.

'It seems to know where it's going.'

At least my circular had done somebody a good turn.

The phone call was from Patrick.

'I see you've lost a white kitten.'

'Yes – I'm sorry.'

'I've had a look, but he's not here.'

'Thanks.'

'Hope he turns up.'

'Yes – so do I.'

He'd let me off lightly and I was very grateful.

Everything seemed to wind down after that. There were no more callers but I still looked out for him. It had become second nature to me to peer in through shed windows and nudge open gates as I walked.

Nick came home for one weekend and then another. Aileen and I worked hard on our books and life returned to normal except that every half-hour or so I took a stroll to the back door to see if Thermal had arrived home unannounced.

'You should have given him a key,' Aileen told me.

And yet if I happened to delay one of my checks for more than five minutes, Aileen would be off across the hall to pull open the door and rattle my eardrums with her whistle.

She had hauled his litter-tray down to the cellar where it wouldn't be a constant reminder. The kitchen seemed much larger without it and one day perhaps, when the memories weren't so sharp, we could convert it into a jacuzzi.

I opened a cupboard one morning and noticed that his vast stockpile of Whiskas had disappeared.

'I gave it to Mrs Barraclough. She took it for her Arnold.'

I assumed that Arnold must be Mrs Barraclough's cat, but knowing Mrs Barraclough it could have been her husband.

Aileen thought she had cleared away all the reminders, but on the night after Thermal's disappearance I had trodden on his sultana as it sat meditating on my office carpet. It was miles away, warming itself by the fan-heater.

I apologized, gave it the kiss of life and pumped it back into some sort of shape. It was now under intensive care in a matchbox by the ashtray on my desk.

I also managed to smuggle a tin of Whiskas beef and kidney into our wire basket as we slalomed our way around the aisles in Sainsbury's. You never know – miracles do happen.

At home Aileen plucked it out of the carrier bag and tried to make sense of the label. She peered at it – the tip of her nose nuzzling the tin.

'What's this?'

'Stewing steak – I thought I could do something interesting with it in an emergency.'

'Oh.'

I stowed the tin away on a top shelf and hoped that she wouldn't feel peckish while I was out.

On his final night in England we took Nick over to the Lodge Hotel at Birkby for a meal. They actually cook their food instead of buying it in boxes from Marks & Spencer and it always makes a nice change for us.

Nick had to be at Manchester Airport by five o'clock in the morning and so we sat up talking until well after two. Aileen had fallen asleep twice already and now she was nodding again.

'Why don't you take her off to bed, Dad? I'll doze in the chair here and then slip out – we can say our goodbyes now.'

That took care of another hour, and then Aileen and I half carried each other upstairs. Nick had settled down in the recliner chair in the study and I knew what he was like – I would stay awake in case he fell asleep.

I dropped off within seconds and the next thing I knew there was a tall figure standing by the side of the bed. It was still dark and my head was floating, but I recognized the voice the moment he spoke.

'I've brought a friend of yours to see you.'

I reached out and switched on the bedside light and then Nick leaned forward and placed a scruffy kitten on my chest. Its earnest little face looked as though it had been daubed with warrior paint and it seemed to be wearing a small combat jacket, camouflaged with streaks of oil and grease.

'Thermal?'

The kitten took a pace forward and fell over. I put a hand either side of him to help him to his feet and they nearly met through the thin body.

'Where've you been?'

From somewhere deep inside his motor started running with a purr that was much stronger than he was. It faltered now and then as though it hadn't been tuned properly, but his enthusiasm kept it going.

, Supported by my hands he took another step forward and touched his forehead softly against mine. Then his legs collapsed and he fell in a heap under my chin.

Aileen struggled to come up from under, but

sleep wasn't letting go of her easily. She tried to look intelligent.

'Is this the er – have you er?' she asked, failing miserably.

'It's Thermal, love – he's come back.'

She needed a little more time and so I turned to Nick who, from his great height, was looking down on the scene like some benign uncle.

'Where did you find him?'

'I put my cases in the car, switched on the engine and then the lights and there he was – lying in the middle of the road exhausted. He was on his way home, but I don't think he'd have made it. He was too weak to stand up.'

The kitten had fallen asleep but he woke as Aileen reached out for him and, then having found him, covered him with her hand.

'Is it Thermal?'

'Yes – Nick found him.'

'He's so thin – he's half
starved.'

The kitten pushed his head
up hard against her hand. It
was that nice lady who trod
on him a lot.

'Come on, my love – let's
get you something to eat.'

That wasn't a bad idea –
he'd been missing for exactly
a month.

Chapter Nine

Aileen led the way downstairs and beat Nick to the kitchen by a short head. I followed at a more sedate pace, cradling Thermal in my arms – I could feel a shoulder-bone hard against my palm, sticking out through his fur like a coathanger. In the kitchen Aileen rattled the milk bottles as she opened the fridge door.

'Up there, Nick, on the top shelf of the cupboard – there's a tin of Whiskas. I can't reach it.'

Why did I think I could fool her? She couldn't see – but she could see through me.

We could almost see through Thermal. Under the fluorescent light his matted coat hung like a rag on the jutting bones and his tail, which had always been something of an apology, now draped itself across my elbow like a piece of string.

Nick searched for the tin of cat food as Aileen poured a dribble of milk into a saucer and then held it under Thermal's nose. He sniffed and dabbed his tongue as though it were all too much trouble for him.

'Come on, love – give it a try.'

I lowered my arm so that his head hung over the saucer. He began to lap, very slowly at first, but then

91

he quickened the pace a little as the liquid lubricated his throat.

'*I remember this stuff – milk isn't it?*'

He readjusted his body so that his head wasn't on sideways any more and began to tackle the job in a more professional manner. The three of us smiled sickly smiles at each other – like the last scene in a Lassie film. He burped loudly and we smiled again.

'I must be off,' Nick said, not moving, 'I shall miss my plane.'

'Yes – you go,' I told him absently. 'You mustn't be late.'

'Mustn't miss it,' said Aileen, wiping the splashes of milk from her hand with an oven glove.

We were mesmerized at the sight of the little tongue darting in and out.

'I'll give it a couple more minutes – see if he eats anything.'

He picked up the tin-opener and Thermal's ears flapped as it bit into the lid – it was one of his favourite sounds. Aileen arranged a slight morsel, *nouvelle-cuisine* style, on the side of the saucer and placed it under his nose.

The kitten who began to nibble at the outer edges was a very tired kitten indeed, but then, as he worked his way into the middle and the Whiskas hit the spot, his fur became more alert and his ears swivelled independently – it was his trademark and a very good sign.

'*That was very pleasant – any more?*'

Aileen refilled the saucer, a little more generously this time and the kitten wriggled in my arms.

'*If you don't mind – I need to get down and use*

my feet for this one.'

I put him down on the floor and he tucked in. Ten minutes later he had finished the whole tin and, in celebration, he tried one of his luxurious stretches, but he wasn't up to it yet and he wobbled slightly and fell over.

'You know – I think we might rear him,' said Aileen as she scooped him up and gave him a big cuddle. 'If he doesn't explode during the night.'

We made a hollow for him in the duvet and he slept between us. We didn't sleep – not for a while anyway. Daylight was already creeping in through the window, but we slipped the Teasmade on to manual and had a final cup of tea and a cigarette while we indulged in a long awaited spot of kitten watching.

'I missed him.'

'So did I,' muttered Aileen, both her hands cupped around the hot tea like a child's.

'Silly, isn't it.'

'How do you mean?'

'Well look at him.'

He looked like something out of Dickens – a ragamuffin. Fagin would have thought twice about taking this one on – he would have let the side down. His coat didn't fit him any more and it was filthy. He must have been locked in a garage somewhere – he hadn't merely brushed against the grease, it had massaged itself into his fur.

The state of his paws suggested that he had spent the last month changing the sparking plugs on an ancient Ford Escort and around his mouth there was an oily tidemark that suggested he had acquired a taste for the stuff.

'He looks like a very small motor-mechanic.'

'More like Al Jolson,' Aileen suggested.

She leaned forward and covered him with her hand, triggering off a purr that came up deep and resonant out of the hollow.

We should have put a cloth down – the duvet would never be the same.

'He reminds me of one of my dad's pipecleaners – they were disgusting.' I switched off the bedside light and we settled down.

'He's lovely, isn't he?'

'Yes.'

I rang the vet first thing the next morning. He sounded as rough as I did.

'What's he doing now?'

'Fast asleep on the bed.'

'That's the best thing for him – he'll know what to do. They're tough little devils, you know. When he's had a rest bring him in, I'll give him the once-over.'

'Right.'

'Just one word of warning.'

'What's that?'

'Don't give him too much to eat straight off – little and often, that's the way. It's common sense really.'

'Yes, of course.'

I put the phone down and nipped upstairs to see whether he was really fast asleep or whether I'd killed him.

★   ★   ★

He had left the bed and come looking for us, but the stairs must have seemed like the north face of the Eiger to him and so he had pitched his tent on the top step and curled himself up into a ball.

He was fast asleep but he managed to open one eye as I carried him downstairs.

'Hello – Deric, isn't it?'

'Yes – how are you feeling now?'

He didn't say – he was fast asleep again, so I parked him on the rug in front of the fire and he slept away the afternoon while I worked on the book.

We worked well. By the time Aileen arrived home at tea-time I had four pages under my belt and Thermal had shuffled his way through at least a dozen of the more generally accepted sleeping positions, and added to his repertoire another three that had never before been attempted outside the circus.

'We're home.'

Aileen stood in the hall festooned with the parcels and carrier bags of all nations. Christmas was coming and there was a festive air about her as she moved slowly across the hall like a human flypaper.

I poked boxes out from under her arms and un-hooked bags from her fingers and gradually she began to appear to me in sections.

'You're not to look in that one.'

It was a Do-It-All carrier bag and I tried not to look disappointed. My hobby was avoiding doing any of it.

'Where's Anna?'

'She's coming – with the rest.'

Anna had arrived one day as a financial adviser. Since then she had also become shopping adviser, fashion consultant and friend. She was young and beautiful and bossy as hell.

She came up the stairs completely obscured by a large igloo that had been cut in half and lined with fur.

'What the hell's that?'

'It's for Thermal – it's a cat-bed.'

Aileen and I sat on the floor, drinking tea and watching Thermal twitch on the hearth rug.

At least he seemed to have regained enough energy to relive the nightmares of the past month. Some of the more powerful shockwaves drove his little body across on to the carpet and every now and then they were accompanied by a plaintive cry that had us wincing.

One such wave brought him shakily to his feet and then he tried to clear his head and work out whatever it was that had just happened. He didn't move for a moment, he stood still – his head bowed, like a small starved donkey waiting to be taken to a sanctuary.

Two short paces took him to the fireplace and then, very systematically, he began to lick the stonework.

We watched in fascinated horror as his tongue covered stone after stone, his head angling so that he could take the horizontal mortar in one long sweep.

He was still in his garage, or wherever he had been imprisoned – this was how he had survived,

licking the moisture from the
walls and harvesting protein
as he went.

At the far end he reached a
speaker built into the fireplace
and this surprised him – he
hadn't seen this before.

'What is it?' Aileen asked.
'What's he doing?'

Her voice startled him and he
flattened his body to the ground. Then turning his
head he saw us and sat up like a stone lion, his
eyes burning bright.

Then they went out again. He must be seeing
things. He sank down until his chin rested on the
floor and he watched us as though not believing we
were really there.

'It's all right – you're home now.'

I went over and picked him up and for a few
moments he just lay there, not moving. Then I felt
his claws reach through my sweater and touch my
skin.

'You're safe now.'

I stroked him very gently and he hutched up a
little until his head was tucked up under my chin.
Best place he could have been.

He chose Marmite for his starter and then followed
it with two helpings of turkey as his main course –
to hell with the vet, what did he know?

Sensibly he declined the chocolate pudding – a little
too rich for him right now he thought – and rounded

off the meal with a drop of milk and warm water to settle his stomach.

He didn't offer to wash up and so I had my hands in soapy water when I remembered his litter-tray. He might need that. I dried my hands and hauled it up from the cellar.

Slotted back in place it looked even bigger than ever now and made the kitchen seem much smaller – it was what they call a feature.

The fur igloo stood in the hall looking awkward and embarrassed as though it wasn't quite sure what it was supposed to do. It was backed with a pale blue material, but the fur fabric itself was that startling sort of blue much favoured by fairground teddy bears in Blackpool. It didn't match a single piece of furniture in the house – thank God.

I carried it into Aileen's study and sat it down in front of her.

'Do you want to see if he'll take to it?'

'Oh yes – look here, Thermal.'

He looked and for a moment he thought they'd come for him. I pushed it over towards his hearth rug and he backed off and longed for the safety of his garage.

But after a while, when it still hadn't attacked him and he had begun to realize just how ridiculous it was, he stepped off his rug and had a good sniff at it.

'What colour is it?' Aileen wanted to know. 'Is it blue?'

'Yes – I've never seen anything quite so blue in my life.'

'The carpet's green, isn't it?'

'Yes.'

'Still – they put blue and green together these days, don't they?'

'Some people do, yes,' I agreed and made a mental note to strangle Anna the next time I saw her.

In the meantime Thermal had become more adventurous and was trying to climb inside it. I was very proud of him and gave him a helping hand with a little push under his bottom.

He turned around a couple of times and then sat there undecided, cocooned in fake fur. It was a straight choice between taste and comfort and I knew my Thermal – he was a discriminating little kitten who instinctively knew when things were right. It had rubbed off from me.

He turned around once more and then with a sigh settled down to sleep, his scruffy little body melting into the blue nylon tufts.

'I'm ashamed of you.'

He peered over the parapet and gave me one of his looks.

'It's a damn sight more comfortable than that bloody thing you bought me.'

He didn't use to swear – he had coarsened somewhat while he was away.

Chapter Ten

Mrs Crampton came to do for us on Wednesday morning and by Wednesday afternoon I was swearing that one of these days I was going to do for Mrs Crampton. She came to hoover here and there, dust here and there, and spread despondency here, there and everywhere.

This was only her third week and already I had known her a lifetime.

'We've got to get rid of her.'

'We can't – not while she's still depressed.'

Mrs Crampton had been depressed ever since the 21st of December 1982 when, at half past eleven that evening, her husband Harold had told her that the mince pies she had bought from Marks & Spencer were a damn sight better than the ones she made herself.

It's the sort of remark that just might get up your nose if you have always fancied yourself as a dab hand with pastry, but it's not really enough to form the basis of a five-year depression.

It was the following March before she spoke to him again and the truce that followed was an uneasy truce, shadowed as it was by the thought that things could never be the same again.

Now, in the run-up to the fifth Christmas, the

memory still burned bright, and over the past two weeks I had learned more about Harold, mince pies and Mrs Crampton than I ever wished to know.

Aileen had decided it would be a nice idea to have the Christmas tree in the hall this year.

'We'll have all the presents underneath.'

Thermal thought it was a great idea. I had been giving him regular runs around the courtyard to make sure he knew his way about and he loved the trees out there. He had sharpened his claws on them and climbed up them and fallen out of them and he was quite overwhelmed.

As he watched us put the tree together he rubbed round my ankles and expressed his appreciation.

'This is awfully good of you – I don't deserve it really. I shan't need to go out at all now.'

I soon put him right. I picked him up and delivered a short sharp lecture on the subject.

'Now you're not to go anywhere near it.'

'It's pointless telling him that,' said Aileen, 'you know what he's like.'

'He understands more than you think.'

Thermal nodded in agreement. He was reaching that age when he could be trusted to act in a responsible manner – he wasn't a kitten any more.

She picked him up and gave him a cuddle.

'He's only a kitten.'

He snuggled his head under her chin and stuck his nose inside her sweater. Being a kitten wasn't that bad really – maybe he'd give it a few more years.

We were sorting out the decorations when a rather damp Mrs Crampton arrived.

Aileen was in her study uncomplicating a string of Chinese lanterns and I was hard at work, strapping a splint to the wing of a crippled angel. Thermal had just dragged the one-legged fairy under the hostess trolley and was about to have his way with her.

Mrs Crampton took off her wet coat and slung it over the telephone table.

'They shed needles all over the place,' she grumbled as she stuck a sliced loaf under her coat, 'and I know who'll have to hoover it up.'

'It's plastic,' I told her, 'it's artificial.'

'They're just as bad,' she said, marching off into the kitchen, 'they get everywhere they do.'

Thermal poked his head out from under the trolley at the sound of a strange voice.

'Who was that?'

'Mrs Crampton.'

'Who?'

'Mrs Crampton – you haven't met her yet.'

'I can't hear you,' shouted Mrs Crampton from the kitchen, 'you'll have to come in here if you want to . . . my God, what's that?'

She was staring in horror at the litter-tray.

'It's for the cat.'

'You haven't got a cat.'

'Yes we have.'

'I've never seen one.'

'Good morning,' welcomed Thermal as he strode into the kitchen, *'I don't believe we've met.'*

She relaxed slightly at the sight of him. The size of the litter-tray must have led her to believe that we were harbouring an undernourished leopard.

'He'd disappeared before you started,' I told her, 'he came back at the weekend.'

'*So you don't have to worry any more,*' Thermal assured her.

She folded her arms and sized him up. His coat still hung loosely like an ill-fitting anorak and he'd spread the oil and grease with his tongue now, so that he had about him the grey, anonymous look of a technical college lecturer.

'I can't stand cats,' she said, 'they shed everywhere. I can't be doing with cats.'

I tried to keep him out of her way but she seemed to go looking for him. He still needed his rest, but no sooner had he collapsed in front of a radiator than in would come Mrs Crampton and before he knew where he was he was half-way up an attachment and heading tail-first for the dustbag.

She also told tales. Every ten minutes or so she would burst into my office with a cushion under her arm.

'Just look at the cat hairs on this – it's disgusting. You want to keep him off the furniture.'

I brought him into the office to keep him away from her and he sat on my desk and watched me type.

'*I remember doing this before – it's all coming back to me now.*'

I remembered as well – remembered him sitting

there, explaining in fine detail the workings of a writer's office to his friend the sultana.

'I've got a surprise for you – what about this?'

I picked up the matchbox from beside the ashtray and slowly pushed open the drawer. He stuck his nose inside and sniffed.

'*What?*'

I tipped it upside down and his friend the sultana fell out. The rest seemed to have worked wonders for the wizened little grape and he sat on my blotter looking plump and refreshed. If anything he had fared better than Thermal, who still looked thin and pale – but then he was supposed to be a white kitten.

They were delighted to see one another again and charged all over the desk – Thermal the playful aggressor, the sultana pretending to be frightened. They must have got the idea from watching Aileen and me.

I found it difficult to work against the whining of the hoover as it thumped its way around the hall. Mrs Crampton had a bad effect on the hoover and it went through a personality change while in her charge – it attacked skirting-boards and doors.

Instant freedom had also slightly deranged the sultana – it was over-excited and even Thermal looked embarrassed at its behaviour.

I gave up and went to finish off the Christmas tree. Thermal and his little friend came along to give me moral support, but thankfully Mrs Crampton had now ploughed her way through the hall and had gone off to burn the stubble in the drawing-room.

Aileen had taken a cup of coffee into the bathroom

to listen to Radio Leeds. Since she can't see to switch from station to station she has half a dozen sets in half a dozen rooms already tuned to different wavelengths. The bedroom is equipped with the World Service and her study rejoices to the sounds of Radio Four. She spends much of her time running round the house like somebody not quite right, but this morning she had spent ten minutes on the toilet with Martin Kelner and she emerged eager to discuss the vital issues of the day.

'There's a woman on the radio complaining because she says there's a lack of variety in the Christmas presents you can buy for your cat.'

'That's ridiculous.'

'Isn't it just?'

'It's a pity they haven't something better to think about.'

'They want locking up.'

'I think so.'

There is nothing more satisfying than the cut and thrust of an intellectual debate, and so it was with a satisfied smile on her face that she went back to her study, ready now to sample the headier heights of Radio Four, having practised on the nursery slopes with Martin Kelner.

And she left me with a problem. After that little exchange – how was I going to give Thermal his tin of salmon on Christmas morning? It was already wrapped in festive paper, a rather nice design, I thought, with a little bunny in wellingtons and a bobble hat and it was lying under the Christmas tree along with the two ping-pong balls, the cat-nip mouse and a quarter of the onion and chive cheese to which he'd taken such a fancy.

I would just have to get up that bit earlier, then the two of us could open our presents together before we took Aileen her morning cup of tea.

I stood back and admired my handiwork. There's no doubt I have a way with me when it comes to decorating Christmas trees. I could make a living at it, if it wasn't such a seasonal occupation.

The one-legged fairy smiled down at me from the very top. It was her turn this year, the crippled angel had the job last Christmas and it was only fair that they should take it in turns.

She'd slipped a bit – one-legged fairies do tend to slip a bit, they can't get a proper purchase and need their horizontal hold adjusting from time to time.

I climbed up the steps and reached out for her and she moved slightly – not a lot, just a nod of the head and a flick of the wand, but it was enough to make me pull my hand back.

She moved again, this time performing the perfect pirouette, a movement for which one-legged fairies have a natural advantage, and then she half-turned, bent over with her back to me and lifted her skirt. I was at the top of a pair of steps and a one-legged fairy was mooning at me.

The fairy began to rise, slowly, until she was standing almost proud of the Christmas tree. A branch rustled just below her and I leaned forward and stared in and there was this kitten's face staring out at me –

he had all four legs wrapped around the trunk and he was hanging on for dear life.

I don't know which of us was the most surprised. He was, I suppose – he gave me a sickly grin which soon turned into a sickly grimace as the tree tottered and began to fall sideways.

The steps went with it and we fell together, side by side, and to make it worse I had this stupid kitten looking at me all the way down.

I hit the sideboard. I don't know where Thermal landed – somewhere painful I hoped, and then all hell was let loose as Mrs Crampton burst into the hall from one direction and Aileen from the other.

'What's happened?'

'He's been playing silly buggers,' Mrs Crampton told her in a voice thick with satisfaction.

Aileen knelt down and spoke tenderly to a square block of solid wood.

'Are you all right?'

'I'm at this end,' I told her and she came over.

'Are you all right?'

'I'm fine,' I said, sliding out sideways from under the tree. 'Just be careful you don't . . .'

There was a crunch from somewhere near my left ear.

'. . . tread on any of the decorations.'

There were baubles everywhere. Broken baubles, cracked baubles, baubles that had been smashed into

a hundred pieces and, scattered all about Aileen's end of the hall, baubles that had been freshly ground into a fine powder.

'You've broken this as well,' said Mrs Crampton, trying not to look smug and failing miserably.

'No,' I told her, 'that only had one leg to start with.'

I found Thermal in the bathroom. He was hiding by the toilet, sitting next to the lavatory brush. It was a good hiding place – you could hardly tell them apart.

'It's all right, come on – no hard feelings.'

'I'll just stay here for a bit if you don't mind.'

'OK – when you're ready.'

We cleared up the hall between us. I was in charge of raising and refurbishing the tree, Aileen was in charge of the dustpan and brush and Mrs Crampton charged about with the hoover and grumbled continuously.

'I told you they made a mess.'

'It's worth it though, isn't it?' said Aileen. 'When it's all finished.'

Mrs Crampton looked at her in astonishment. The thought had never occurred to her and she went off to the toilet to mull it over.

'If you find a sultana,' I said to Aileen, 'it's Thermal's.'

'Right,' she said, peering into her dustpan, her nose hard up against the handle. 'I'll look out for it.'

If the sultana was still within hearing range it must have made him feel a lot better.

We had just decided to break off for a cup of tea

when Mrs Crampton screamed. It was the sort of scream you scream when you're sitting on the toilet and a cat you didn't know was there pushes its paw underneath your bottom.

'That's it,' she yelled, 'I've had enough – I'm going and I'm not coming back.'

Thermal strolled out of the bathroom behind her.

'Get her to put it in writing.'

'I'm sorry,' said Aileen. 'It must have been a shock.'

'You think more of that cat than you do of me,' muttered Mrs Crampton.

There was a stony silence.

'If you'll give me my money – I'll be off.'

She went and we all breathed a sigh of relief. Aileen sat down on the telephone table.

'She'll be back.'

'Why do you say that?'

'I'm sitting on her sliced loaf.'

I tried to square it off and it looked almost like a loaf again by the time she came back for it.

'I haven't changed my mind,' she shouted as she marched into the hall, 'I left my . . .'

She put her head round the kitchen door.

'. . . what are you playing at?'

It was a fair question. We had emptied the fluff from the hoover bag and spread it on newspapers until the kitchen floor looked like a badly insulated loft.

Aileen was on her hands and knees at one end and I was sifting my way towards her from the other.

Thermal was sitting in the middle of the pile, turning it over to let it breathe.

'We're looking for Thermal's sultana,' I told her.

Chapter Eleven

Aileen pushed her plate away and reached out tentatively for her glass of wine. I had cooked the turkey to perfection at 190 degrees for one hour and ten minutes – just like it said on the Marks & Spencer's box. She leaned back, lit a cigarette and I waited for the compliments to gush forth.

'Read yours first.'

'Right.'

I picked up the paper and found the stars. I am a Sagittarian and we are wonderful people. Lovable, kind, considerate, dashing – a bit dodgy when it comes to financial matters, but that only serves to make us even more lovable. It hurts us when our cooking goes uncomplimented, but we don't make a fuss.

'What's mine say?'

I read Aileen's for her. Aileen is a Virgo but she cheats. She says she has Aquarius rising and if Virgo doesn't suit she will try Aquarius instead. Virgo didn't suit.

'I'm more an Aquarius really.'

I read Aquarius, leaving out the bit about keeping a close eye on loved ones who were going through a funny phase. It was a little better than Virgo but not much.

'He's not as good as Patric Walker is he?'

'Not a patch on him.'

We Sagittarians don't like to make waves and so I didn't point out that he had done very well by me, especially the bit about my creative genius.

I pushed the ashtray towards her and moved the sugar bowl out of reach, it would save a lot of time spent sugar sifting later on. Every evening the after-dinner routine is the same. Wash the pots and dry the pots and put the pots away. Then, finally – examine the sugar for any little black bits.

She leaned forward and very carefully flicked her cigarette ash into a small bowl of mixed nuts.

'What was that noise?'

'I didn't hear anything.'

'Listen.'

I listened and heard a loud crunching noise as it floated past me on its way from the kitchen.

'That's Thermal – he's having his lunch.'

'What's he eating? Is it Go-Cat?'

'No – I bought him Brekkies this time.'

'Well they're much louder than Go-Cat. I can't usually hear him from here.'

Neither could I, and so after moving the mixed nuts up to the far end of the table and screwing the top back on the jar of cranberry sauce, just to be on the safe side, I went off to investigate.

Thermal was just finishing his third glass bauble. He spat out the metal bit by which you attach them to the Christmas tree and then burped.

'What the hell are you doing?'

He looked up, burped once more, and then calmly knocked another bauble down from one of the lower branches.

'*A little HP Sauce wouldn't go amiss.*'

I snatched the glass ball away from him and picked up the collection of metal pins from around his feet.

'You're not supposed to eat them.'

'*Don't be ridiculous.*'

I waved the bauble under his nose and he licked his lips in anticipation.

'These are expensive – they don't grow on trees you know.'

His little brow furrowed – he didn't seem to understand that, and I wasn't too sure about it myself, so I tried to put it another way. It would be best to reason with him – to get him on my side.

'Do that again and I'll break your neck.'

Reasoning seemed to work. He took a long hard look at me and then drew himself up to his full height, which isn't all that impressive when you are only six inches tall. Then he turned on his heels and marched into the bathroom.

'It's no good sulking,' I shouted after him, but he took no notice and so I turned my attention to the tree.

I moved all the baubles up a notch and brought the candles and the baby crackers down to those lower branches that were within kitten-mauling height. I didn't mind him sucking the odd candle.

It took a few minutes to re-create the perfect symmetry I had achieved on my first run. If I'd wanted the baby crackers on the bottom branch I would have put them there in the first place, but it looked all right, and then my attention was diverted by a strange rolling noise coming from the bathroom.

It sounded something like a sledge running out of control down a long grassy bank, neither of which we had in the bathroom, and so I pushed open the door and there was Thermal sitting upright on the lavatory seat, pounding the toilet roll into submission with his front paws.

The toilet roll was a blur. It was belting round and round at about thirty miles an hour and a hundred or more sheets of perforated paper were piling up in shreds on the floor.

'Right – that's it.'

I marched towards him and he saw me coming. He stopped pounding and gave me one of his looks. I stopped marching. There was something different about this kitten.

This wasn't the ankle-rubbing sycophant we all knew and loved so well. The kitten sitting there on the toilet seat was no ordinary kitten. The Andrex Kid himself had come to town and he was prepared to take on all comers.

It was a stand-off between me and a pound and a half of lean muscle. For Thermal it was a sit-off. He stared back at me.

'A kitten has to do what a kitten has to do.'

I moved towards him and he shifted slightly, his tail twitching.

'Go ahead punk – make my day.'

I sat down on the edge of the bath and waited for him to make his move. His eyes were blue as the sea and as hard as nails and they never left mine as his body unfolded itself and landed, light as a whisker, on the pedestal mat.

There was a swagger in his hips as he slowly made his way towards the door, paws strutting, jaw jutting. Even his little backside was on the alert and seemed to be operating as a third eye.

It watched me all the way to the airing cupboard and then his head turned and his lip curled as he sneered over his shoulder.

'Wipe your bum on that then.'

I chased him right across the hall, up two flights of stairs and twice round the landing before he shot off into the back bedroom and hid under the bed.

'Come on out.'

'No – you've spoilt it all now.'

When I woke up the next morning he was fast asleep on Aileen's chest and not mine – being out of favour had its good points and for once I was able to have breakfast in peace.

I ran out of milk somewhere around the fourth cup of tea. As I pushed open the back door to bring in a newly laid bottle the most beautiful tortoiseshell cat in the world nodded a polite good morning and walked into the hall.

It was a girl – there was no doubt about that. I am not very good at sexing rabbits – we once had a rabbit by the name of Ronald who gave birth to triplets under my very nose – and children under the age of five confuse me unless they are colour coded in pink or blue. But this cat walked like a catwalk model, wearing her fur coat as easily as most women would wear an old pair of jeans at this time in the morning.

'Oh – this old thing.'

If Thermal was the man from Millets, then here was the girl from Givenchy.

I wished I had tidied the place up, or at least put a comb through my hair. She paused at the foot of the stairs and looked about her – one paw slightly raised in an elegant gesture.

'I'm sorry the place is such a mess.'

Her eyes swept over me and she forgave me. Such things weren't important to her. She walked over to the far door and went in.

'This must be the drawing-room.'

'Yes.'

We had spent a lot of money on this room and we were very proud of it.

'I could do things with this.'

She was small and delicate, but she seemed to be wearing high heels – there was a coltish look about her that gave her extra inches. She would be about a year old, but elegance and confidence made her whatever age she wanted to be.

'And this?'

'That's my office.'

She wrinkled her nose as she put her head round

116

the door. I tidy it once a year when I've finished a book and I was only halfway through one. She gave me an indulgent smile and turned on her heels.

'What have we here?'

'That's Aileen's office,' I told her and she strolled in.

'Ah!'

She took a tour of the book-lined shelves, the two desks and the hi-tech equipment. She sat on the arm of the recliner chair and had a practice lie on the hearth rug.

'Now I could work here.'

She sat on the fax machine and examined the view from the window, then admired the tidiness of the out-tray and the emptiness of the in-tray before gliding back into the hall.

'What else?'

I showed her the rest of the floor. She only poked her nose round the kitchen door – kitchens were where other people worked and had nothing to do with her.

'Thank you for your time.'

Her fur was a fusion of glossy black and startling white and cinnamon. Well it certainly wasn't ginger – this cat would rather be found dead in the gutter than be caught wearing ginger. It was the colour of autumn – like Aileen's hair.

'I'll be going now.'

I opened the back door and let her out. She paused on the balcony and examined her nails.

'I'll let you know.'

'Thank you for calling.'

'My pleasure.'

*   *   *

Thermal and Aileen tumbled out of bed about an hour later. They came downstairs together and then split in the hall, the kitten shambling sleepily towards the kitchen and his breakfast, the woman peeling off towards her office – she has her breakfast delivered.

I fed them both. Thermal stood in the middle of his bowl and ate all around him, then he lifted his rear-end slightly and ate underneath him. I took my coffee and joined Aileen – her conversation at this time in the morning wouldn't be any better, but her table manners would be a distinct improvement.

I read the *Independent* on the floor and Aileen stared into space. This is what they call togetherness and it lasted for about ten minutes until she switched on the radio. I can't take the excitement of radio early in the morning, I need to be bored gently into the rhythm of the day – which is why I take the *Independent*.

Thermal was nowhere to be seen which wasn't surprising. He has a series of windows that he likes to look out of first thing in the morning – he takes them in a specific order and doesn't like his routine upset. He would be in my office at about quarter past.

I opened the fridge door to put the butter away and it was then that I noticed. I was surprised that I hadn't noticed before. The handle was sticky and the door was covered in blood.

The floor was sticky as well. Whatever this was it was running down the door in rivulets and dripping on to the kitchen carpet. But slowly, like – well just like blood.

'Aileen, come and look at this.'

She came but she didn't look. She felt with her fingertips.

'What do you think it is?'

She put her fingertips to her mouth and tasted.

'It tastes sweet – it's very nice actually.'

I couldn't do that. I could see it and it looked like blood, but I sniffed and it smelt like nothing I had ever smelt.

'Where can it be from?'

'Don't know.'

I trod on something about the size of a gull's egg and since I don't come across gulls' eggs on the kitchen carpet all that often I bent down and picked it up. It was a cork from a wine bottle – a red-stained cork.

Well a nod's as good as a wink to me and I turned to the wine rack. The bottles are stacked horizontally, just tilted slightly towards the business end and pointed straight at the fridge door.

Now hot on the trail I held an impromptu identity parade. Although the bottles looked very much alike from that angle, it wasn't long before I was able to pinpoint the guilty party. It was cowering on the bottom rack with its mouth wide open, blood still dripping from its fangs. I pulled it, kicking and screaming, out of the line-up and arrested it. It was a damson 1986 – the most violent of all the homemade wines.

I remembered this bottle. I had taken part in an outside broadcast in Derby a couple of weeks earlier. The audience were lovely and afterwards one of their number had come forward and said some very nice things about me. He also gave me a bottle of wine and told me that his name was Derrick Ayre. How nice of him I thought. What a warm and wonderful person.

'It's pretty strong,' he said, 'be careful with it.'

I wished I had him there with me now. I had the cork in one hand and if I had had Derrick Ayre in the other there would be no prizes for guessing what I would have done with the cork.

I cleaned up the mess and made to throw the bottle away. There was about an inch of wine left in the bottom and I poured it into a glass. Aileen tried it first and licked her lips.

'It was very good of him really.'

I tasted the wine and it was very pleasant. I began to wish I had licked the fridge door and the carpet.

'Yes it was.'

We drank a toast to him. He wasn't to know that they were exploding damsons, unless of course he was a member of the IRA and was planning to claim responsibility afterwards.

I worked all morning, re-reading the pages I had written yesterday. I hadn't slept very well the night before for worrying about them and now I could see why. They didn't work, and so I took a deep breath, pressed the cut key on the Amstrad, and they disappeared from my life for ever.

I read back even further and scrapped another three pages. I was now back to where I had started out last

Wednesday morning. They say that the ability to be so ruthless is the mark of the true professional – it could also denote a singular lack of talent.

Aileen had been on the phone all morning, talking to her agent, her publishers, the gas board and practically everybody in West Yorkshire. She loves the phone. She isn't blind when she's on one end of a telephone line, it's a great equalizer. It's more than that – she has the advantage, because she can read your voice as effectively as a graphologist will read your handwriting.

She shouted to me and I went to see what she wanted – we have a certain pecking order in our house and I know my place.

'Have you seen Thermal?'

'No – not since breakfast.'

This was serious. His stomach has a built-in alarm system and it never fails.

'See if you can find him.'

I didn't have to look. At that moment he staggered into the study sideways and banged his head on the door frame. His eyes revolved as he leaned uncertainly against the skirting-board and he shook his head as though it didn't belong to him.

And it didn't look as though it belonged to him. He had turned into a pale pink kitten from top to toe and he was stoned right out of his mind.

Chapter Twelve

Thermal jammed his hip up against the wall to steady himself while he tried to get his bearings. Then somebody moved the skirting-board and he was off, lurching across the carpet towards the hearth rug.

'It's all right, Aileen – he's back.'

'Oh good.'

'I'm not so sure about that.'

He wasn't going to make it to the hearth rug. He took the pretty route round by the wastepaper basket – turn left at the coffee table, under the desk, run smack into the video and then ask.

He swayed slightly and then began to back out of a cul-de-sac by the filing cabinet. Viewed head-on he was now a pretty, if somewhat streaky, pastel pink – but the rear-end that emerged from under the desk was painted in such a vivid scarlet that it would have had those monkeys at the zoo going green with envy.

'Where is he?'

'He's here, by my foot.'

Two eyes looked up at me and tried desperately to focus. He must have read my mind because he sat down, stuck his leg up in the air and tried to lick his bottom. It didn't work and he fell over in a heap, his head on my foot.

'*Help.*'

Aileen stood up and came over, trying not to tread on him in the process.

'What's the matter – is he all right?'

'He's just a bit off colour, that's all.'

She picked him up and plonked him on her shoulder where she could see him.

'He's all sticky.'

'It's the damson wine. He must have been standing by the fridge when it exploded.'

He had conquered his fear of the fridge and now spent a large proportion of his day staring at it and wondering why there wasn't a cat-flap in the door.

'His bottom's *very* sticky.'

'He hasn't got round to that yet.'

She took him over to the window where she could see him better and peered closely at his head.

'Is he pink?'

'Yes – you should see the other end.'

'It's stuck to my sleeve.'

We peeled him off and laid him on the hearth rug. I spread a sheet of newspaper underneath him but he didn't know much about it – he was out to the wide.

'Do you think this happens to other cats?'

'I shouldn't think so.'

He woke up five hours later with a hangover and tottered into my office with the middle pages of the *Independent* stuck to his side like a billboard.

'*What happened?*'

'It's a long story.'

I sat him in the sink and washed him down with

Fairy Liquid. It's supposed to be kind to the hands and I hoped it would be just as kind to paws and whiskers and bums. He struggled but he wasn't really up to it.

'Mind my eyes.'

'Shut up.'

'I beg your pardon?'

'It'll go in your mouth.'

'Yuk.'

'See – I told you.'

Aileen wasn't too happy about him being washed. People don't wash cats, she said.

I could remember saying exactly the same thing to my mother the first time I watched her scrub Whisky in the sink.

'My mother used to say she was just dipping him – like they do sheep.'

'It doesn't seem right somehow.'

'Listen to the woman.'

'What do you suggest?'

'Lots of hot coffee and walk him round the yard?'

'Take no notice of her.'

The water was a dull plum colour when I lifted him out, but he still looked like a raspberry ripple. I dried him off and the towel came out in sympathy.

'I *will* take him outside for a minute – give him some fresh air.'

Unfortunately for Thermal we had an audience and, much worse than that, it happened to be a large tom-cat called Denton.

Denton is the school bully. He's built like a bullock

and fancies himself as a villain from the old cowboy days. He dresses completely in black from head to paw.

I have often thought of introducing Denton to some of man's recent innovations such as the machine-gun or the air-to-ground missile. Somebody must love him, though for the life of me I can't understand why – he has the personality of a hyena but none of the charm.

In stark contrast Thermal looked like a designer-kitten as he hopped down the steps to the courtyard. There was just the faintest touch of a Busby Berkeley musical about the scene, as the pale winter sun picked out the pale-pink kitten tripping lightly down the staircase, and only a moron would have failed to appreciate it.

Denton wouldn't have appreciated it as he lay in ambush under the hydrangeas – he was more of a Rugby League man himself.

Thermal sat down on a paving stone, closed his eyes and wondered why his head hadn't come down the steps with him. Should he go and fetch it? No, he was better off without it.

I watched from the balcony as he weaved his way towards his favourite burial ground where the soil was soft and you could do things in private.

He was just about to squat in the shade of a long-suffering azalea when he saw the dark shape of Denton lurking not more than a couple of yards away, and his battered little brain went into overdrive.

'That must be a cat – my mother told me about them.'

He had probably only ever seen half a dozen

cats in the whole of his short life. There was his sainted mother, of course, and his unmarried sister in Brighouse. His father was apparently on active service in the Persian Gulf and Thermal had yet to be introduced. His brother Gordon was away at boarding school. Then there were the three dustbin loungers I had pointed out to him from an upstairs window, but that must have seemed like a lifetime ago.

'I'll go and have a chat with him – make myself known.'

He strolled, quite casually, over to the hydrangeas and smiled broadly at the accident that was about to happen. It was then that I spotted Denton as he shifted slightly and licked his lips. I shouted a warning.

'No!'

The kitten stopped in his tracks, then turned and looked up at me.

'I'm not going to hurt him.'

He didn't stand a chance. By the time my feet hit the courtyard, Denton had finished with him and Thermal lay in a crumpled heap on the paving stones. His ear was bleeding and his fur had been rearranged.

But it was his innocence that had taken the cruellest beating. He hadn't tried to run away. He couldn't believe that this was happening to him, that anyone would want to do this to him. And so he just lay there, wide eyed on the stone slab, and tried to understand.

Denton sat on the high wall and slipped his claws back in their holster. That had taught the kid a thing or two – shown him who was boss. Pink kittens indeed – this gay-bashing certainly gave you an appetite.

He looked so damned pleased with himself that I threw a piece of mortar at him, but he didn't even bother moving. Just eased his head to one side and watched it sail past.

'One day I'll have you.'

'Don't hold your breath.'

It hadn't been a good day for Thermal – it had been the sort of day you could do without. But at least he had the pleasure of telling Aileen all about it.

'There were three of them – weren't there?'

'Yes.'

'Enormous they were.'

'Huge.'

'Especially the black one.'

'He was the worst.'

'I showed him though – didn't I?'

'You did that.'

Then the tortoiseshell cat walked into the study and Thermal panicked and hid behind the wastepaper basket.

She was just as beautiful as I remembered and I introduced her to Aileen. They got on famously and set off on a tour of the bedrooms. A head peeped out from under the desk.

'Is it safe?'

'Yes.'

'Who was that?'

'I don't know – she calls in occasionally.'

This time she stayed

longer. She was surprised to see Thermal.

'I didn't know you had a cat.'

'Yes – this is Thermal.'

He was too shy to say anything. He just sat there with a stupid grin on his face and simpered. She took the initiative – she was that sort of cat. She glided over to him and they touched noses. Her eyes watered.

'Does he drink?'

'It was an accident.'

She made herself at home and stretched out on the hearth rug. Thermal didn't know what to make of it. His unmarried sister in Brighouse, by all accounts, is a much plainer woman and he'd never seen anything quite like this before.

He stumped around for a while, pretending he had a limp, and then when that didn't bring him the sort of attention he was after he went all silly and did his funny walk on the mantelpiece.

When he fell off it made his ear bleed again but Aileen made a fuss of him and so, with his ego charged a little, he felt confident enough to go and lie down beside his new friend on the hearth rug.

Not *right* beside her you understand – at a bit of an angle and slightly to the rear, so that if he was snubbed he could brush it off lightly.

We watched a cassette of Victoria Wood's one-woman show. She's Thermal's favourite and she cheered him up enormously. The battle with Denton had done him no good at all and it obviously hurt him when he laughed. So he just smiled his thin little smile

128

every now and again. All the same, I'm sure it did him a world of good.

We wound the video back and played the song about the hostess trolley once more, he loves that, and then Aileen zapped the television with her remote control. She's lethal with it.

'I think she ought to go home now.'

'I don't know where she lives.'

'*She* does.'

I couldn't argue with that, we shouldn't be encouraging her to stay. I showed her to the door.

'*Thank you for having me.*'

Her manners were impeccable – so different from those of our own dear Thermal. She slipped quietly down the steps, across the courtyard, and into the lane.

On impulse I followed her. I wanted to know where she came from, and she made it easy for me. She didn't skulk in the dark shadows by the wall. She walked right down the middle of the narrow lane as though she were leading a parade.

I didn't want to alarm her, so I tried to make myself as inconspicuous as possible. I was brought up on the films of the fifties and I knew exactly how a private detective would go about it.

I could have done with a trench coat and a hat-brim to pull down, but we private dicks have to improvise. So I stuck my hands deep in my pockets and kicked aimlessly at pebbles as I walked along.

Just to make doubly sure, I perfected a tuneless whistle and kept my eyes firmly on the ground. I was just another ordinary guy on these mean city streets.

It worked beautifully. She had no idea she was being followed. She stopped a couple of times and so did I, pretending to examine the privet hedge for any trace of Dutch elm disease – just a trick of the trade.

She was getting too far ahead of me now, and then suddenly she turned into an open gateway – I didn't know which one. I sprinted after her and she was waiting for me on the wall.

'Come on – we haven't got all night.'

She wriggled through the bars of the rickety gate and made her way up the garden path to an old stone cottage. I leaned on the wall and watched as she settled down on the back step. It seemed out of character – I would almost have bet money on her having her own key.

Of course this could just be another of her calls and not where she lived at all. I heard footsteps behind me, and the sort of old man you always refer to as an elderly gentleman stopped at my elbow.

'Can I help you?'

'I was just watching the cat.'

'Oh she's back, is she?'

He pushed open the gate and faced me from the other side.

'She's a roamer is that one.'

'Yes, she's just been to see me.'

He had the tang of best bitter on his breath, and he shifted his foot so that he could use the gate as a bar-rail.

'She's not happy here. It was my daughter's cat, you see, she's gone to Canada with her two lads, so we took it in. Couldn't take it with her.'

The cat was listening as though she knew we were talking about her, and she came a little closer.

'My wife can't stand cats – she's allergic to 'em, you see, but we thought we'd give it a try. She can't be in the same room as a cat and I have to organize 'em so as they don't ever meet up.'

'She's called to see us a couple of times.'

'She will have. She's been in everywhere. I've had her brought back more times than one. I think she's decided she's not stopping here and she's sizing everybody up.'

'Do you think so?'

'I'm sure of it.'

She had certainly given us the once-over. It was as though an estate agent had given her the details.

The cat moved in closer still. A stiff breeze rippled the bushes and it wasn't easy for her to hear from over there. The man bent down and stroked her head.

'Do you want her?'

'I'm not sure – we've got one already.'

'There's a cat-flap goes with her. I bought it when she came but I haven't got round to putting it in yet.'

I was weakening. A couple of months ago I wouldn't have entertained the thought. I had kidnapped Thermal on an impulse – I didn't need the responsibility.

'Tell you what,' he said. 'If she comes to see you again you have my blessing. You don't have to send her back.'

The cat looked up at me.

'It's your move.'

The man looked up at me.

'It'd make my life a lot easier for me.'

It was my move.

'All right then – let's see what she decides. I live in the house on the . . .'

'I know which one's yours – it's that big 'un. You'll have plenty of room over there. I'll bring the cat-flap round when she's made her mind up.'

We shook on it and said good night, but I had only gone about ten yards when the most beautiful tortoiseshell cat in the world sailed past me. The old man still leaned on his garden gate.

'I think you've got yourself a cat.'

She was heading off down the lane as though she wanted to be the first to tell Aileen and Thermal. She hadn't even bothered to pack her pyjamas – I didn't even know her name.

'What do you call her?'

'Her name's Tigger,' he shouted.

Chapter Thirteen

I pushed open the door, very gently so as not to make a noise, and she was lying there, stretched out on the sunbed. She should have been wearing goggles, I suppose, the ultraviolet rays might hurt her eyes, but we only had one pair and Aileen was wearing those.

Unlike Aileen, who was stretched out naked beside her, Tigger had wisely decided to take it in stages and she still had her fur coat pulled tightly around her.

They were both fast asleep, but Tigger opened one eye and yawned as she heard the floorboards creak under the bedside rug.

'It's all right,' I whispered. 'Don't wake up.'

I slipped my hand underneath her and stood her on her feet. She fell over, so I tried again, this time holding on to her and steadying her against Aileen's thigh.

'It won't take a minute.'

I dipped my spare hand into my trouser pocket, but the tape measure was in the other one and so I had to lean forward, bend sideways and cross my left hand over to my right-hand pocket and then, just as my fingers touched the tape measure, something went in my back and it didn't half hurt.

I let go of the cat and sank to my knees. Tigger fell over again and then the door swung open and Thermal marched in.

'What's going on?'

'Shhh!'

'I haven't been in here before.'

'Be quiet – you'll wake Aileen.'

He jumped on the bed and was surprised to see the other two stretched out under the canopy.

'Hello.'

He stood both his front paws on Aileen's stomach and began pounding, as though he were kneading dough.

'She hasn't got any clothes on.'

Aileen stirred, and her half-smile budded into a generous half-moon as he began his massage.

'Mmmm!'

My back eased off slightly and I dug the tape measure out of my pocket. Tigger watched Thermal with interest. For all she knew this was our regular Sunday afternoon routine and she might have to take over one day if he wasn't very well.

She moved in a little closer to study his technique in fine detail, and as she passed by me, I stopped her and took her inside leg measurement.

Three and a quarter inches? That couldn't be right. I tried again and it was. I had no idea she was such a low-slung cat. When she walked across a room it was as though her legs went right up to her nostrils, but then I saw that she had sunk up to her knees in the mattress.

I lifted her on to the bedside table and measured again. Ten and a half inches! That couldn't be right either.

'Stop stretching.'

Some cats are good stretchers. Thermal isn't – at his best he can manage a modest hump-back bridge. But Tigger is the most liquid of cats, and whenever she arches her back she becomes the perfect croquet hoop.

I waited until she came down again and measured once more. Five and a half inches. That seemed about right. I measured again and it had gone up an inch. Aileen was waking up.

'What are you doing?'

'I'm taking Tigger's inside leg measurement.'

'What for?'

'The cat-flap.'

There was a silence as Aileen considered this little nugget of information. I can't stand silences and I have to fill them in. 'That's what it says on the box – that's the way you get it at the right height.'

'What about Thermal – are you going to build him a ramp?'

'He'll grow into it – eventually.'

He was concentrating on her navel now, pulverizing it with smooth, even strokes.

'Not if he doesn't pull his claws in he won't.'

'*Sorry.*'

'That's better.'

With the cat-flap came a booklet on how to train your cat to use it. It was written by 'A well-known consultant on animal behaviour' and it said to put the cat on one side of the flap and a tempting bowl of food on the other. I couldn't help thinking that consultants in animal behaviour get their money very easily.

135

I had fixed the flap in the cellar door. It seemed to make sense – I wasn't going to vandalize a front door that had stood guard for a hundred years, and round at the back I would have had to puncture three doors before the cats could work their way through to the hall. It would have been the Horse of the Year Show for them every time they went in or out.

So the cellar it was. There was already an old settee in there and I pulled it up close to the central-heating boiler so that they could sit round the fire and spin yarns.

I looked around at my handiwork with pride – a few magazines and a kettle and they would want for nothing. They could lounge about in comfort here until I opened the inner door and let them trot upstairs.

What remained of the weekend was devoted to 'on the job training' – an intensive course in cat-flap technology. As was the following week, the rest of the month and a large part of the ensuing year. Even today I still run a regular series of booster courses which have been specifically designed for cats which are, not to put too fine a point on it, as thick as two short planks.

Tigger's objections were on aesthetic grounds. There was no way she was going to bang her head against a plastic flap. It wasn't natural and it was humiliating. Thermal's initial reaction was that it hurt.

I crouched on the cellar side of the flap and wiggled it to demonstrate the general principle. They sat outside and watched. I dropped the flap and waited.

And waited and waited. Twenty minutes later I

lifted the flap and peered through the hole and they had both fallen fast asleep on the step outside.

I took the consultant's advice and placed a bowl of steaming hot fish just inside the door. I waved it under their noses first and Thermal became quite agitated.

Eventually I heard the thundering of hooves and there was an almighty crash as he launched himself at the flap. He only made it halfway and hung there, draped like a condom over the school railings, the plastic flap banging against his head.

I pulled him in and he seemed both excited and bewildered to find that he had actually travelled through a solid door. The problem was – would I always be there to lend a hand?

We tried again – this time with a block of wood either side of the door – and it did help to elevate the shorter legs of the shorter cat. But not enough – his back legs caught at a critical stage and he hung for a moment like a pheasant in a fishmonger's before thrashing himself loose and crash-landing down on the bowl of fish.

A tortoiseshell paw reached under the door and clawed out a sizeable chunk of spilt fish. If I had thought of extending the gap by a couple of inches I wouldn't have had to bother with the flap.

By mid-week I had

acknowledged the fact that I was never going to get the message across on my own and I had taken on an assistant who was well versed in the subject.

Chico Mendes O'Connell is a small ginger tom-cat of nervous disposition. He lives with Bridie just across the lane and had been named after the man who saved the rain forests.

The combination of being born in Yorkshire and raised by an Irishwoman, who had taught him Gaelic from the moment he could walk, had served to give him a rather befuddled air. Being saddled with the name of a Colombian folk hero had proved the final push towards a nervous twitch that would stay with him for life.

He was a friendly little cat and willingly offered his help. Bridie brought him over because he didn't like to cross the lane on his own.

Tigger was having a lie-down in the airing cupboard when he arrived, and so Thermal was able to benefit from a spot of personal tuition. Chico proved to be a natural-born teacher, and if Thermal had proved to be a natural-born pupil we might well have got somewhere.

Aided by his beautiful assistant, Bridie, who was there to give him a helpful shove up the bottom at crucial moments, Chico put on a stunning, paws-on, demonstration of cat-flap agility the like of which had never been seen before – certainly not through our cat-flap.

He showed Thermal the various techniques in slow motion; the paw-on-ledge, the gentle head-butt, the back-leg-thrust, and finally the four-paw-balance and leap. Then he went through his repertoire once again, this time at a tremendous rate of knots, leaping in and out like a gazelle.

Thermal was amazed. He hadn't realized it was an Olympic sport, and he couldn't wait to have a go.

Where he made his mistake was – he shouldn't have taken off sideways. Both nearside paws came through, but nothing else followed. Since most of him was hanging on outside we had to open the door to get at him, and that was when he fell off.

Chico had enjoyed himself thoroughly. The professional in him was more than a little disappointed that he hadn't managed to bring his pupil up to scratch, but he was delighted to find that he hadn't lost his touch.

I paid him in Whiskas and then accompanied him and his lady assistant up the steps. Behind us, in the cellar, we heard a dull thud as Thermal's head hit something rather solid.

The light was fading in the courtyard and Bridie and I didn't see Denton at first, but Chico did, and in the blink of an eyelid had hit the dirt, like a commando, behind a stone in the rockery.

Unlike a commando, Chico wasn't coming out – he had clashed with Denton before and he hadn't enjoyed it one bit. Bridie, however, is made of sterner stuff and she doesn't expect her menfolk to tremble in public.

'Come on out, Chico – remember you're an O'Connell.'

Chico remembered exactly what had happened to more than one O'Connell during the Troubles, and stayed exactly where he was. He also remembered what had happened to Chico Mendes, and he was taking no chances.

As we moved across the courtyard the security lights came on and caught Denton in the beam, like a prisoner about to go over the wire.

I shouted at him and he turned. He was the most evil-looking cat I had ever seen. His fur was constantly on the alert and even his ears had split ends.

'Leave him to me,' muttered Bridie, 'I'll throw something at him.'

'I'll see to him,' I told her. I thought she might throw Chico.

He stood his ground as I moved towards him, and then began to spit as I drew closer. He didn't move until I almost trod on him, and then only because he saw Tigger up on the balcony, staring down at him.

He was up the steps like a shot and racing towards her. I couldn't get there in time and stood mesmerized like a rabbit, watching the scene from below.

He stopped six inches away from her, back arched and breathing fire. He was twice the size of her and spitting out the most terrible threats.

She sat facing him, as calm as a village pond, her whole body at peace with the world.

He spat again, and a shudder of disgust crossed her gentle face. Very slowly she raised one paw, and then, with great deliberation, she placed it right on his nose and pushed.

He sat down with a thump and looked totally bewildered as she stood up, enjoyed a long luxurious stretch, and then wove her way lazily around him before floating down the steps to join us.

Chico fell in love with her at that very moment. From behind his rockery stone he joined in the round of applause as she tripped down off the final step. He would have come out to congratulate her in person, but his leg was playing him up.

She took it all in her stride and gave me a modest smile, then shook her head as she turned to go down the path.

'Men!'

Meanwhile, down in the cellar, there was a small off-white kitten who knew nothing of all this. He was having a battle of his own with a plastic cat-flap and things were not going all that well.

I had forgotten about him, and it was an hour or so later when I went down to see how he was.

'Where have you been?'

'I'm sorry.'

'That thing's stuck.'

'No it isn't – look.' I flipped it open with my finger.

'It was.'

'Well it isn't now.'

'Well it was when I tried it.'

'I'll show you what we'll do.'

I took a couple of clothes-pegs from out of the

basket and tacked one each side of the lid.

'There – it'll stay up now.'

He gave it a try. He jumped out through the hole and then he jumped back in again. Then he jumped out again and peered in at me with a cross little face.

'Why the hell didn't you do that in the first place?'

I tried to make it up to him. I had the car to put away in the garage, so I picked him up and tucked him under my arm.

'Come on.'

'Where are we going?'

'You'll find out.'

I plonked him on the passenger seat, but by the time I arrived round at the driver's door he was up on the rear shelf playing nodding-head Alsatians.

We went once round the block to see how he would take to it and he took to it like a duck to water.

'Can I drive?'

'No.'

He pulled a face through the window at Mrs Bramley's dog Alfred, and then tried to peel the AA sticker from its moorings.

I pulled down the lid of the glove compartment and he jumped in. I slammed it shut and he was as quiet as a mouse until I eased the car into the garage and let him out.

Tigger was sitting on the wall waiting for us. I gave her a wave and set Thermal down on the drive before reaching up for the door. It's an up-and-over door and it's a devil if it's been raining – it holds the water in a vast lake and when you tip it over it's like Zambezi Falls.

No problem today, though – it had been as dry as a bone. I yanked it down, and Denton came flying off the end like an Olympic skier.

It's not true that cats always land on their feet – Denton didn't. He crashed down on to the concrete with a sickening thud, and for a minute he didn't move a muscle.

He must have been sunning himself up there with not a care in the world, and then all of a sudden the earth was pulled from underneath his paws.

He nearly landed on Thermal, but he didn't hang about to take his revenge. As soon as he had gathered his wits together he made for the hills like all good rustlers.

Thermal was totally bemused – he didn't know what had happened – but I thought Tigger was having a hernia over there on the wall.

The battle with Denton was by no means over, but at the moment it stood at two–one to the good guys.

Chapter Fourteen

It was the perfect way to spend a crisp winter's evening. A roaring fire, whisky and water in a crystal glass and a lovely woman stretched out beside me – her head on my lap, the firelight burnishing her hair with the rich glow of copper.

And over there in the easy chair lay a very contented tortoiseshell cat, licking the head of a small stubby kitten who was fast asleep and snoring in stereo.

Although Thermal's Dayglo days were over his fur still had a pinkish cast about it, and now it stood rigidly to attention, in punkish tufts, to mark where the rasping tongue had been at work.

Tigger had slotted in and around the kitten's routine so neatly that it seemed she had always been with us. Thermal's well-regulated lifestyle had simply rolled along as smoothly as it always had. More so in fact – his back-up team had now increased from two to three.

Thermal's love of ritual was getting a bit much. Every time I fed him I had to go through a spiel, extolling the virtues of the dish he was about to receive. When I took a tin of beef and kidney from the cupboard I had to show him the label like a wine waiter. Sometimes I draped a tea-towel over my arm, but he hadn't eaten out all that often and the sarcasm was lost on him. Then I had to launch into my sales pitch.

'This is very highly recommended, Thermal. A recent survey taken amongst doctors at the Royal Free Hospital in London has shown that of all the cats they have treated there for appendicitis the ones to have recovered most quickly from the operation have been those fed on this very same diet of Whiskas beef and kidney. That just shows you.'

He wasn't always easy to please.

'Free hospital did you say?'

'It's just an expression – it's very well thought of. They swear by it at Great Portland Street as well.'

'Oh – all right then.'

Eventually I came up with a line that was a winner each and every time.

'At Buckingham Palace the Queen insists that the corgis be served nothing but this particular recipe of liver and chicken.'

'What's a corgi?'

'It's a sort of Royal cat. Look – there's a picture of one on the tin.'

'Go on then – I'll have it.'

By the time his dish hit the floor he would be drooling. If I just banged it in front of him without a word he wouldn't touch it.

In a round-about way it was Thermal's obsession with routine that caused the accident, and perhaps the worst moment of all was having to explain to Doctor Helen exactly how it had happened.

She's a good friend and she's very easy to talk to, she makes me feel better the moment I walk in the surgery – but even so . . .

'Were you doing any heavy lifting work?'

'Not exactly – no.'

'What were you doing?'

She would have to know – never mind what she thought of me afterwards.

'I was lifting the cat up, so that it could play with the bathroom light switch, when it went.'

Surely she would understand. She had cats herself, and the last time I saw them they were doing disgusting things to one another – and in the kitchen at that.

'How do you mean – the cat went?'

'No, the cat didn't go – my elbow went. When I lifted him up to play with the light switch.'

'Tell me exactly what happened.'

'I dropped the cat.'

'Did it hurt?'

'Do you mean me or the cat?'

Eventually we sorted out exactly what I *did* mean and she asked me if the pain persisted or whether it ebbed and flowed.

'The pain disappeared after a few minutes, but then it came back the next day.'

'When?'

'When I lifted the cat up to play with the light switch again.'

She considered the matter for a few moments.

'Is it a particularly heavy cat?'

'No – I've got him in the car if you would like to have a look at him.'

She decided against it and gave me a prescription.

'And I suggest you don't lift the cat up to play with the light switch for a few days.'

That was easier said than done. Thermal and I have established another ritual at bedtime. Aileen and I work until the early hours, anywhere between half past one and four o'clock. The phone doesn't ring and the television doesn't tempt – it's perfect, but Thermal is much younger than we are and he needs his sleep.

So at midnight he tucks into a plate of something tasty and then goes and stands behind the kitchen door. I push a feather through the crack and wiggle it up and down and he chews it and bites it and thumps it with his paws until it's dead.

Then we go and bank up the fire and he goes through his coke-sniffing routine until he feels I can manage on my own – and then he goes and sits in the bath.

I chuck the rest of the coke on the fire and go and join him. Not in the bath – I sit at the side and turn the taps on. He has a good drink and when he's had his fill he goes and sits under the light switch. It's a long cord that dangles halfway down the wall and I lift him up so that he has both front paws free and he knocks the living daylights out of it for about five minutes.

It takes it out of him – burns up his surplus energy, which is what it's all about – and then he lies back on my shoulder and we have a bit of a cuddle. Not too much, you understand – after all, we are both blokes.

Then I put him down and he walks over to his rug by the radiator. The fur igloo has long since been relegated to the cellar – it's now a sort of guest bedroom if you like, for when he or Tigger have any of their mates round to stay the night.

He curls up tight and I tell him a bedtime story – nothing too complicated, we don't want his brain racing at this time of night – and then he settles down and I tell him what a good boy he's been.

You know – more or less what everyone does with their cat at night.

So you can imagine what a shock it was to his system when my elbow went and I dropped him. He lay where he landed and looked up at me.

'No – you've got it all wrong. That's not supposed to happen.'

It seemed to throw him completely, and he nipped back into the kitchen and hid behind the door.

'No – we've had that.'

So he went back and sat in the bath and it was ages before I got him to sleep. In the morning he'd taken it out on the toilet roll again – it was all over the place. I was a bit annoyed about that because I didn't sleep much either, but I didn't take it out on the toilet roll.

I took it out on Thermal instead. I ignored him completely and he doesn't like that. It seemed to work because he immediately moved into his 'cute kitten mode', which involves lying on his back a lot looking up adoringly, and a certain amount of ankle butting.

He made a good job of it and it wasn't too long before I melted, and then he was able to move on to stage two, which basically boils down to the fine art of walking away just as your owner bends down to stroke you.

Timing is everything here, and if a kitten gets it spot on, then the owner should be left with his knees bent, his arm outstretched and his fingers brushing thin air as a disdainful tail, just out of reach, runs up the flagpole and semaphores 'up yours' to the world in general.

Thermal got it spot on, but I didn't rise to the bait. It was a time to make allowances, a time to be kind and understanding – because I knew that I was taking him to see the vet later that morning and he didn't.

It was that time in a kitten's life when we humans decide that it would be better in the long run. My mother once put it beautifully. Her cat Whisky sat on the hearth rug looking as though life were just not worth the living any more.

'What's the matter with him?'

'He's been to the vet.'

'What for?'

'I've had him orchestrated.'

So Thermal was to be orchestrated, and I felt lousy about it. He was so excited when I opened the car door. He jumped in and started off by savaging the AA sticker, a job he hadn't been able to finish on his first trip. But then he soon settled down and sat between the two front seats, studiously watching my feet on the pedals and making mental notes for when he started his driving lessons.

I had a cardboard box ready on the back seat. It had 'Fruit Salad × 12' written on the lid, but that was only to lull him into a false sense of security. There was a fluffy towel secreted in the bottom and the box was actually a cat transporter in disguise.

But that was for later and in the meantime he could play at Nigel Mansells while I popped in to see Doctor Helen.

When I came out he was fast asleep in the box. Why do they do this to us? If I'd had to catch him, wrestle with him and then force him into the box I could have justified my actions.

'Don't be so stupid – it's for your own good.'

But this way he was making me feel as though I was about to shoot a prisoner who had come from out of the bushes with his arms above his head and given himself up. I pushed down the four flaps and tried to live with it.

At the vet's I sat between a woman nursing a stuck-up Siamese in a custom-built cat basket and a man with a tortoise in a British Home Stores carrier bag. The cat was extremely well bred and about as interesting as the tortoise.

Across by the fish tank a young man sat with a very small box on his knee. On the side of the box was written, '6 chocolate éclairs'.

What had he got in it? Stick insects? A miniature gerbil?

I was fascinated and couldn't help myself.

'Excuse me. I couldn't help wondering – what have you got in your box?'

He looked across at me and then he looked down at his box.

'Half a dozen chocolate éclairs.'

'Right – thank you.'

Why do I make such a fool of myself? Why do I never learn? But at least I could redeem myself.

'Brought them in for their injections have you?'

'How do you mean?'

'It was just a joke.'

'Oh – I see.'

I was saved by a lady in a white coat leading a rather tense little terrier out from the back. It shared an owner with the chocolate éclairs.

'We'd like to see Harold again in a week's time, Mr Wolfenden, just to make sure.'

Harold – what a stupid name for a dog. I wondered what he called the éclairs?

The lady in the white coat released an index card from her clipboard.

'Thermal Longden?'

'That's me – or rather, it's him.'

'This way please.'

It was the first time I had admitted to Thermal

in public, and as I paraded my cardboard box through the crowded waiting-room I rather wished I'd called him Harold instead.

The vet peeled back the cardboard flaps and revealed his potential victim having a great big stretch and a yawn.

He stood him on a table and the kitten looked much smaller than I remembered.

'You're a fine little fellow, aren't you?'

'Yes.'

'Has somebody been painting him?'

'It was an accident.'

'It was damson wine – he got in the way. It's nearly faded now.'

'He must have looked quite spectacular.'

'He's a nice man, isn't he?'

'Yes he did.'

'Aren't you going to introduce us?'

I felt wretched as I drove away. My trouble is – I take things too much to heart. I know it doesn't make sense. In a couple of days he would be as right as rain and have forgotten all about it and it was certainly for the best.

Even so. He was such a trusting little devil. He had made an instant friend of the man who was about to cut off his bits and pieces, and as I crept out of the surgery his purr was rattling the instruments on the trolley.

I felt as though I had just introduced the Marathon Man to Laurence Olivier.

*   *   *

When I picked him up that evening he was still out like a light. The vet assured me that all was well.

'He'll be back to his old self in a day or so.'

It was about midnight before he came round. I sat on the arm of the easy chair and stroked his head.

'It's all right – you're home now.'

His eyes were rolling as he tried to focus on my face and I rubbed the back of my hand against his ear. Aileen was kneeling down on the hearth rug in front of him and Tigger was sitting anxiously on the other arm. He needed his friends around him at a time like this.

He ignored the other two and turned the dizzy eyes on me. I suppose it was only natural – we had a special bond between us. After all, I was the one who had rescued him – the one who had brought him in from the cold.

He was too weak to purr but the eyes steadied themselves and held me in their gaze. There was such a warmth in those eyes and such a depth of feeling.

'*You bastard,*' they said, '*you bastard.*'

Chapter Fifteen

He was back on his feet in no time, but it was a little longer before the news of *my* reprieve came through.

Then a couple of days later, sitting in my office, I heard the sound that brings a knowing smile to the face of any cat owner – the unmistakable click of a table-tennis ball as it rattles against a skirting-board.

It wasn't Tigger. She was here with me, riding on top of the photocopier as I printed out my manuscript. And yet every time I went off to investigate, Thermal would be lying on his blanket by the fire, reliving the hell that I had put him through – the rolling eyes thick with delirium, the low moan escaping from between parched lips.

'No, not the knife – anything but that.'

Eventually I caught him out. He was trying to bend a free-kick round the leg of the sideboard. He'd seen Paul Gascoigne do it on *Match of the Day* and he wasn't going to let a Geordie get the better of him.

He took it quickly and left the three-pin plug completely wrong-footed as the ball took a slight deflection off the base of the standard lamp.

He had already set off on his lap of honour when he heard my roar of approval from the doorway. To his credit he didn't even look up – he just collapsed in a heap by the coffee table, clutching his paw to his side.

'*Aaaghh.*'

One has to be fair, and I would wait to see the televised replay before making a final decision. All the same, I reckoned I could force a draw out of this one.

It was Tigger who brought the sweetness and light back into the house. She was on her morning rounds and she couldn't understand how she'd missed it before, it must have been there for ages.

I was flushing the toilet for Thermal when she came in. We had done a lot of toilet flushing in the good old days before light switch bashing had taken over. Now light switch bashing had been relegated to the bloodsports section and toilets were back in vogue again.

Thermal had taken to it like a duck to water, right from the beginning, and although he still wore his disdain like a suit of armour, he couldn't hide the knot of anticipation that began to unwind in his stomach as his front paws hooked over the pan and I took a grip on the handle.

I thought he would have been put off for life a long time ago when the toilet seat fell on the back of his neck – but no. He seemed to accept that this was one of the risks you had to take if you were going to be a dedicated flushing fanatic.

As I pressed the handle down, he tensed with excitement – he loves the split second of silence when nothing happens – and then he shifted position slightly as the water roared and swirled. He waited with breath bated and paws trembling as first the water disappeared and then, with mounting excitement, he leapt on the seat and stuck his head inside to watch as the pan filled up again.

The calm that followed brought exasperation with it.

'Pull it again, kid.'

He knew very well that you can't do that – not straightaway, but the lull in the proceedings reminded him that he wasn't supposed to be friends with me any more, and he jumped down in disgust.

He almost landed on Tigger, who had discovered an intruder lurking between the Harpic and the lavatory brush.

'What have you found?'

Tigger ignored him. It wasn't moving and it could be dead, but she wasn't taking any chances. She could have a battle on her hands here.

'What is it?'

Tigger brought her head round and gave him one of her looks – one of those she keeps in the freezer.

'Sorry – I'll keep quiet, shall I?'

She set herself. Weight perfectly distributed, head still, rear-end swaying, slowly at first and then winding itself up as the moment of truth came closer.

'I won't say another word.'

She sat down again and closed her eyes in exasperation.

'Sorry.'

'What is it, Tigger?'

Thermal gave me one of *his* looks – one of those he keeps especially for me.

'*Shush – be quiet.*'

'Sorry.'

He slipped in behind Tigger – just to let her know that he was there if she needed him. Then he looked back over his shoulder at me.

'*Amateurs.*'

She went for it when we least expected it – least of all the sultana.

The Harpic went flying, the lavatory brush did a somersault and the sultana came out between her back legs like a rocket. It hit Thermal in the chest and he was up on the toilet seat before he could say . . .

'*Ralph!*'

He couldn't believe it. Tigger turned the sultana over on to its back with her paw and gave a sigh of disappointment. Still, you had to take these things seriously. You never knew whether these little devils were going to be armed or not – better to be safe than sorry.

'*It's Ralph.*'

Thermal leapt down and
crouched beside the sultana.
There was love in his eyes and
adoration in his paws as he
gently pushed it this way and
that.

Tigger didn't know what to
make of it and I was going
to find it hard to explain the

situation to her. We had combed Mrs Crampton's hoover fluff until our lungs were full of the stuff and all the time the sultana had been trapped behind the lavatory.

Thermal banged his head against Tigger's thigh and then came over and gave my ankle a polish.

'Thank you.'

'It was nothing – really.'

'I was talking to Tigger.'

He went back to the sultana and lay down beside it.

'Now – if you don't mind – we would like to be alone for a few moments.'

We left him to it and went to put the kettle on. Tigger took a drink of milk from her saucer then looked up at me.

'Ralph?'

'It's a new one on me.'

For the next seven days it was Disneyworld revisited. The sweetness and light pervaded all four corners of the house, there was love and there was devotion, and it was as boring as hell.

The two cats curled up all day together, sharing a communal blanket with a sultana who couldn't wipe the smile off his face.

I shared a blanket with Aileen, but that was a different matter – people who work late into the night need a little time to themselves in the afternoon. But if we left them for just a moment or so, all three of them would come trooping upstairs after us.

'We're a family you see.'

It wasn't easy to bring that certain smile to Aileen's

158

face with a couple of cats crouched affectionately, one on each pillow, and a smug little sultana grinning a demented grin at me from a dent in the duvet.

I began closing the bedroom door, something we hadn't had to do since the children left home. But it didn't work – you could hear the splinters flying as the two cats pounded away at the woodwork and then the ominous silence as the sultana measured up for a tunnel.

'I can't take any more of this.'

'Just relax,' Aileen breathed sexily in my ear, 'and ignore them.'

'I can't – I don't want Thermal to find out what he's missing.'

He found out soon enough. A gradual sea-change swept over Tigger. At first it manifested itself in the form of gentle affection – she would roll over on to her back at the sign of the slightest footfall and ask for her tummy to be rubbed. I thought it was all rather sweet until it hardened into a raw passion as she squatted down and stuck her bottom in the air every time Thermal hove into view.

He was panic stricken, and had to lock himself in the airing cupboard as his Disneyworld quickly whipped itself up into *9½ Weeks*. I told Aileen what was happening.

'Ah,' she said. 'She's on heat.'

'Well I don't like it – and what's more Thermal doesn't like it.'

'Well the pair of you had better get used to it.'

★   ★   ★

It went on for ages – she was disgusting, and Thermal spent more and more time over at Chico's across the lane.

I couldn't lie on the rug first thing in the morning and read my *Independent*, Tigger would roll all over it and go bananas.

I couldn't cope with it. It's bad enough when Aileen's like that. At least Aileen doesn't do it out in the yard when I'm paying the milkman – or at least if she does, I haven't seen her.

For Thermal came the added disadvantage of finding every tom-cat from miles around queuing up on his doorstep. Every time he put his head out of the door he got mugged. And when Chico, who hadn't been seen to and who was too young to see to it himself, came over to find out what all the fuss was about – he got mugged as well.

I began to let Thermal out through the cat-flap in the cellar so that he could give them the slip. It worked for a while, but then one day Tigger slipped out with him and he was almost trampled to death in the rush.

He came in with a look of pure disgust on his face. He shuddered and sat down on the rug.

'Anyone who can fancy Denton ought to be put down.'

Eventually, after what seemed like a decade or so, she calmed down and became, once again, the Tigger we all knew and loved and not the Tigger that every other tom-cat in the district was trying to get to know and love.

Thermal and I called a conference and decided to

invite Aileen. She came reluctantly – she knew what it was about.

'I think we ought to take her to the vet,' I began.

'*Hear, hear!*'

Aileen hesitated. She was up to here with tom-cats queuing on the steps, and she had been driven mad by the constant revving of their motorcycles in the back lane. Still, she hesitated.

'Why don't we let her have just one set of kittens?'

'*That's sexist, that is.*'

'They should have one set of kittens,' she insisted.

'*She's got me.*'

Right or wrong I was on Thermal's side in this one, and we had rigged the voting before the meeting started.

'I think we should get it over with.'

'*Doesn't hurt much – makes your eyes water a bit, that's all.*'

It did more than make Tigger's eyes water – it laid her out for a week. She lay slumped on the hearth rug and Aileen held a saucer of warm milk under her nose.

'I can't believe she was pregnant already.'

'Well she was.'

'Poor Tigger.'

'Just think – we could have had lots of little Dentons running all over the place.'

Thermal shuddered at the thought and hoisted his back leg up around his neck.

'I wonder which one the father was – it could have been Ranji, he almost pitched a tent . . .'

We both fell silent at the same time – made speechless by Thermal's astonishing display of athleticism as his tongue reached places I didn't even know he had.

He always made a feature out of washing his bottom, but we'd never seen him do it on the mantelpiece before.

He could feel the silence being aimed at him and paused in mid-lick.

'What?'

'Nothing.'

'Yes there was.'

'We were just wondering who the father was.'

'Well it's no good looking at me . . .'

A little row of daggers crossed over from the mantelpiece and caught me smack in the eye.

'. . . is it?'

Chapter Sixteen

We were very busy over the next few weeks. I had reached that magical moment – chapter thirteen – when, for no known reason, the writing becomes easy and the book seems to take off on its own.

Aileen had reached chapter fourteen, when, for no known reason, it becomes ever so bloody hard again and you feel like bursting into tears.

Tigger took over the running of the household in general and of Thermal in particular. What he needed, she decided, was a loving mother and a firm hand. She had been within a whisker of having kittens of her own and she was determined to give him the benefit of her experience.

Thermal was having none of it – he was determined to make his own way in this world and had formed a small public relations consultancy in partnership with Chico Mendes O'Connell from across the lane. They had started out with very little in the way of venture capital and were extremely short on experience, but their enthusiasm knew no bounds and already they had landed a two-house contract.

On the strength of that, they opened a small office in the cellar from where they ran the whole operation. PR was the coming thing and they were determined to be in on the ground floor – or even better, the cellar.

Their job was to make all visitors to either house feel especially welcome – to create an oasis of goodwill and then watch the benefits flow.

The men who came to empty the dustbins had been the first to taste the techniques employed by the two entrepreneurs.

'The bins are over there in that shed.'

'I'm afraid this door sticks a bit.'

'I think you'll find there's another bag over there in that corner.'

'Excuse me – you've dropped some potato peelings.'

They had already earned a pat on the head, a ride each on a rough shoulder, an over-ripe chicken carcass, a get–out–from–under–my–bloody–feet and a for–God's–sake–bugger–off.

This was all within the first week. The future beckoned and the sky was the limit.

On Monday morning Thermal had a working breakfast with Chico over at Bridie's place and then came back at just after twenty-five minutes past eight for elevenses.

The next seven days had been designated 'Welcome the postman week' and meticulous planning was the order of the day. They could have done with a wallchart, but capital expenditure of that magnitude was out of the question, so they had to play it by ear.

Thinking wasn't Chico's strong point, it wore him out, and so he had a nap in the office while Thermal took first watch on top of the gate in the garden wall.

Viewed from the lane the wall is just above head height, but from down in the courtyard it stands a good fifteen feet tall. Seven stone steps reach up to a stone balcony, surrounded by an elegant iron rail that I'm going to get round to painting one of these days.

It must have been the best part of an hour later when, from the kitchen window, I saw the postman plodding along the lane, his eyes down, examining a clutch of letters in his hand.

Thermal saw him coming at the same time, but was torn between the dictates of his chosen profession and the natural-born instincts of a cat.

He should have stuck his paw out and said, '*Hi there. My name is Thermal – let's do lunch.*'

But a sophisticated kitten–about–town must never look too excited and so he half stood up, had a good stretch with his head low down and his bum stuck up in the air and then pretended to notice an interesting splinter in the top of the gate.

He gave it a bored little sniff. It was up to the postman to make the first move. He should have said, 'Hullo there, Thermal – and how are you, old chap?' Then if Thermal had wanted to ignore him, he could have done so – to devastating effect.

Cats rarely make the first move because they hate being ignored themselves, but the postman didn't know this, and he had his eyes firmly on the letters as he put his shoulder to the gate and sent Thermal spinning off into mid-air, fifteen feet above the ground.

He knocked on the door a few minutes later and delivered several letters for Aileen, a bill from the garage for me and an extremely indignant kitten who appeared to be suffering more from acute outrage than anything else.

'Did you see that?'

'It was your own fault.'

'You cannot be serious.'

'You shouldn't show off.'

'I don't believe I'm hearing this.'

Tigger took pity on him and tried to lead him away to the crèche she had established behind the television set. Thermal had other things on his mind.

'Gerroff.'

She listened to his protests with a gentle smile and all the annoying doorstep-patience of a Jehovah's Witness. She tried again.

'Gerroff!'

He bounced off down to the cellar to wake Chico and tell him that their business had just collapsed around their ears and Aileen went off to read her letters through the scanner.

Tigger sighed and gave me a rub round the ankles before going off to do the thousand and one things a mother has to do.

She'd win him round yet, with unquestioning love, patience and tolerance. She would win him round – or break every bone in his body in the attempt.

As the full horror of the garage bill sank into my unwilling mind I wondered if Tigger would like to go round there and sort them out first.

Aileen appeared at my side with a letter in her hand and the sort of look on her face that tries to be a very modest sort of look indeed and doesn't quite manage it.

'Read that.'

It was an invitation to the Women of the Year Luncheon at the Savoy Hotel in London.

'That's terrific.'

'And now that.'

It was page two of the letter and it informed Miss Aileen Armitage, novelist of this parish, that she was on a shortlist of six for the Women of the Year's Frink Award.

'That's wonderful.'

'I can't believe it.'

'It's true enough.'

'Read it to me.'

The scanner allows Aileen to absorb the sense of a message – one large letter at a time on the computer screen. But the effort takes away most of the flavour and so I read it out aloud to her, in my best BBC voice – the one where I try very hard to sound like an announcer and don't quite manage it.

'Of course I shan't win it.'

'No – of course you won't.'

'You rotten devil.'

She took the letter from me and smoothed it with her hand, but you couldn't have smoothed that smile from her face with a steam iron.

'I'm very proud of you – they couldn't have made a better choice.'

'Thanks – I shall just go and enjoy the day.'

167

'Right.'

'Whether I win or not.'

'That's the spirit.'

She turned to leave, legs moving but not needed as she floated above the shagpile.

'And let's not tell anyone – not yet.'

'If that's what you want.'

She disappeared back into her office and within thirty seconds my phone on the branch line gave a little ding – like it does when she phones her youngest daughter to tell her the good news. I popped my head around her door.

'We won't tell a soul – right?'

'It's only Annie – just family and friends.'

I went back to work and made a mental note not to breathe a word of this to any of our deadly enemies.

That night we celebrated in style at an Italian restaurant. A friend had recommended the place.

'Cost you around fifteen pounds a head.'

'Sounds good.'

He must have had a soup and a sweet and a bottle of paraffin – the garage bill seemed quite reasonable

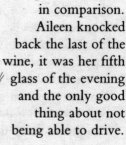

in comparison.

Aileen knocked back the last of the wine, it was her fifth glass of the evening and the only good thing about not being able to drive.

'I'll just pop to the toilet while you pay the bill.'

'OK.'

I guided her over to the appropriate door. We've got it down to a fine art now – I hold her hand and, with a series of well-practised squeezes, steer her to the right, to the left or straight ahead. A stranger wouldn't know that she couldn't see and we just seem to be a very affectionate couple – which we are. Left to her own devices she tends to mingle with a lot of gentlemen who happen to have their hands full at the moment.

The return journey is something she prefers to turn into an adventure. She memorizes the twists and turns, the steps and stairs, and sets out staring straight ahead with a confident smile. Sometimes she doesn't quite make it and I have to move in quickly.

Once she asked a rubber plant for directions, and once she walked straight through a plate glass window. Tonight the course could have been made for her, the going was firm and I would have bet money on her.

Back at the table the proprietor brought the bill on a silver tray. I smiled at the man, choked at the bill and reached for my credit card.

It wasn't there. It had been – I had put it there, in my top pocket. No need for a wallet or cheque-book tonight – just slip my card in my top pocket.

'Shall I need any money?'

'No love – I've got my card.'

But I hadn't. I knew where it was – it was on the windowsill in the bathroom, right next to the

Royal Overseas League shower cap and just in front
of the little bottle of shampoo from The Royal Hotel
in Scarborough.

I walked over to the desk in the corner wearing a
pale grey face that made my white shirt seem almost
colourful. The proprietor didn't seem to notice.

'You enjoya your meal?'

'Very much thank you – but I'm afraid I've come
without my Access card.'

'Of course'a we take Access. We take'a everything. We take'a Barclaycard, American Express,
Diners Card . . .'

'I haven't any of them.'

'Thena we take'a cheque – if you have banker's
card.'

'It's at home – with my cheque-book.'

'We take'a cash.'

'I haven't any cash, but . . .'

His son came over and much as I enjoyed *The
Godfather* I didn't really want to meet him in person.

'Thisa man,' said Poppa, spreading his arms wide,
'he hasa no money.'

'I have'a the money,' I told him, 'but I leave
it at home.'

The son gave me a hard look to see if I was taking
the mickey out of his Poppa. I wasn't and I wouldn't,
but I have this problem. Ten minutes after getting off
the train in Newcastle and I'm speaking like a Geordie.
I sprouted a pair of mental leather shorts in Austria,

and in Switzerland I had learned to yodel before we cleared customs.

'What'a we do with him?' asked Poppa.

I also have another problem. Whenever I am accused of anything, I look guilty.

At school, I used to blush like mad and go all shifty whenever the teacher asked who wrote the rude word on the blackboard. It never *was* me, but I was the one who always got thumped for it.

This time I was going to get thumped by the Mafia, who were certain to make a better job of it than Miss Urton ever did when I was in 4c. The son moved in close.

'Why you not tell us you got no money before you eat?'

'I didn't know then. Look I can . . .'

Poppa and son spoke in rapid Italian, their arms conducting some invisible Milan Philharmonic Orchestra. As far as I could gather, Poppa wanted to send for the police whereas the son was all for disembowelling me with the butter scraper he was waving in his right hand.

Then Aileen appeared, hips swinging as though she was on casters, her red-gold hair freshly combed and a big dob of lipstick on the end of her nose.

'Ready?'

'I can't pay the bill – I've left my credit card at home.'

'Oh well,' she turned to Poppa, 'we'll send it on to you.'

Poppa must have fallen in love with her during the soup.

'Excuse'a me,' he murmured, and with a white damask napkin dabbed at the lipstick on her nose. 'Isa no hurry – any time.'

'We'll post it first thing in the morning.'

I glanced at the son to see if he intended holding me hostage until the cheque cleared, but his eyes were on Aileen's hair. I thanked him for trusting us.

'I would trust the lady with my life,' he snorted.

'What nice people,' said Aileen as we slid through the swing doors.

'Come again,' shouted Poppa.

As we climbed in the car I told her that at one point I thought they were going to duff me up.

'I thought they were charming,' she said

We had only gone about three miles when I looked at the petrol gauge. It was the flashing orange light that caught my attention.

'Need some petrol,' I said, and pulled on to the garage forecourt.

I filled it up. £19.27 it came to and then I walked up to the night-time security window to pay for it.

Must get a receipt this time, I thought – I always forget.

'£19.27,' said the Pakistani attendant, flashing me a great big smile.

I froze completely.

'I've lost my credit card,' I told him, 'and I think I've lost my memory as well.'

The smile vanished.

'You have no money?' He glanced across the office

172

to where an Alsatian the size of a rhino was demolishing a plate of Pedigree Chum.

'Just a second,' I said, and in a daze walked over to the car. I pulled open the passenger door and was met by the raw power of Aileen's vocal cords as she sang along with Eric Clapton.

'Sorry about this, love – how are you with Pakistanis?'

'How do you mean?'

'Never mind – just give your hair a brush and come with me.'

Chapter Seventeen

Thermal is the sort of cat who needs to be up and doing, and without his business interests to keep him occupied he looked absolutely lost.

He assumed the role of guide-kitten once more, but it only lasted a morning. He wasn't cut out for good works and you could hardly call it a career. The pay was lousy and Aileen kept treading on him.

Tigger was fast becoming the Mother Teresa of the family and seemed to have taken over the lease on the cellar, which she planned to open as a refuge for poor unfortunates.

'Come home with me. You'll have a square meal, a warm bed for the night and a couple of quid in your pocket when you leave.'

Word soon went round and her first customer limped down the cellar steps just before breakfast the following morning.

His bedraggled black coat hung loosely from his shoulders and fitted only where it touched. His tail and undercarriage had terminal moth and he had about him that haunted look often worn by those who have suffered the mental wear and tear of living alongside humans.

I was put in charge of the catering while Tigger

made sure he had the cellar to himself.

Chico was allowed to use the place as a sort of halfway house as he waited for Bridie to come home from the shops, but Denton only made it halfway through the cat-flap before Mother Teresa sorted him out with a stiff left jab.

I took my job seriously and did my best to provide a balanced diet for Tigger's patient, but I soon learned that there was no room for gratitude on the menu. He had been given a hard time by the two-legged variety and he wasn't about to trust this one just because he had a bowl of liver and chicken Whiskas in his hand.

I learned to look only at Tigger as I entered the cellar – to talk only to her and pretend that the ragged stranger was invisible. He would stiffen and I could see him mapping out an escape route to the cat-flap, but as long as I didn't try anything stupid, like being friendly, he would stay where he was.

Tigger revelled in her charity work and dreamed of the day when her cellar would be featured in the *Independent* magazine, complete with black and white photographs and solemn text.

She thought she might advertise with a leaflet drop around the outlying villages, but I soon put a stop to that by telling her that we would need planning permission first.

I reported back to Aileen and she peeped in through the cellar window with her binoculars.

'I can't see him.'

'His back-end's sticking out from behind the central-heating boiler.'

'Where's the boiler?'

She always tried so hard to see for herself the scenes that I described to her.

'I can see something.'

She could see an upturned shovel fast asleep by the lawnmower.

'It's not moving.'

Well it wouldn't – would it?

'Listen – that's him,' I told her.

The old black cat had a clipped, northern mew – short and to the point.

'That's only half a mew.'

So we called him Arfur – Arfur Mew. And then we upmarketed it to Arthur. He was a no-nonsense cat and couldn't be doing with anything so twee.

Aileen thought he might be dyslexic, but then she couldn't see him. There were no prizes for guessing what was wrong with Arthur. Somewhere along the line he had broken his tail and both his back legs. They had mended in a fashion, probably under a hedge somewhere, but the tail was now bent like a shepherd's crook and the legs were thin and rickety.

He walked with a sideways stagger and needed the whole of the cellar floor for a turning circle. He had once been a fine cat, a ladies' man – but now he had an air of defeat about him and was probably way behind with his alimony payments.

Thermal wasn't too happy with the arrangements

and I can't say I blame him. Every time he wanted to use his little patch round behind the rhubarb, he would have to wait until Arthur had finished with it and attempted to leave it as he would have wished to find it. Thermal spent hours gritting his teeth and hoping that he would remember to pull the chain.

One morning Thermal disappeared somewhere around half past six. I had stopped worrying about him now, he knew his way around, but when he didn't arrive home for lunch the old fears began to surface.

Normally the stroke of noon would find him licking his lips as he strolled up the steps towards the back door.

'I think I could just fancy a nice chop today.'

Perhaps the stroke of noon is a slight exaggeration. Let's say – give or take seven seconds either way.

But here it was almost five o'clock and still there was no sign of him – I pulled a jacket from the peg and went looking. Tigger was on her way back down the lane – it must have been her day for the Samaritans.

'Have you seen Thermal?'

'No.'

She turned round and came with me. She did garage roofs and high walls, I did shed doors and coal bunkers, but there was no sign of him.

I know it seems pretty stupid to be so worried so early in the day, but after being imprisoned for a month in a garage he tended to keep very close to home. No day trips, no nights out with the lads. You

could set your clock by him – within seven seconds or so.

Tigger found him down by the park. He was sitting on the branch of a tree fifteen feet above the road and to judge from the look on his face he didn't think it was a very good idea any more. He had no idea how he was going to get down and I had no idea how he had got up there in the first place.

The tree is unclimbable – it has a wire cage round the trunk and is as slippery as hell. Even the squirrels give it a miss – a kitten would need crampons, a rope and a long ladder just to reach the first branch.

'I'm going for the ladder.'

'I'll keep an eye on him.'

'I don't think he's going anywhere.'

I am perfectly at home on the bottom two rungs of a ladder. I can hold on with just the one hand and even lean back a bit, but from there on upwards my nose begins to bleed and my knees go weak.

When the top of that ladder is swaying along with the branch of a tree and the foot of the ladder is planted firmly in the middle of a busy road then my whole body goes weak and even my knees feel like bleeding.

A little old man arrived on the scene and he

leaned against the tree trunk as I began to climb.

'You could send for the Fire Brigade you know – that's what they're there for.'

'Well, it's not really, is it?'

'Course it is – they rescue cats and dogs that have got themselves stuck up trees.'

I can't remember ever having seen a dog stuck up a tree, but it was comforting to have him around and he certainly came up trumps with the six traffic cones he placed around the foot of the ladder.

Whether or not he should have removed them from around the North Eastern Gas Board's mobile pump is open to question.

'Will you be much longer?'

'I'm doing my best.'

'Only they'll be shut soon.'

'Who will?'

'The chemist's – I'll be wheezing all night.'

'I'll run you round in the car.'

You feel good when you have gone hurtling through the fear barrier and come out safely on the other side. I felt a strong bond with Chris Bonnington, and Thermal felt like something to eat, so we both had a bite and then lay on the rug together and relived our adventure.

'It was high up, wasn't it?'

'Yes – were you frightened?'

'No – were you?'

'No.'

Aileen had gone over to Manchester with Anna, but Tigger came and sat with us and pretended to be impressed as we lied about how brave we had been. We were men and it was our privilege.

I have always got on extremely well with animals. I get on well with human beings, in fact some of my best friends are human beings, but I have always had a special relationship with our furred and feathered friends.

When I am with people I am always aware of the enormous intellectual gap between them and me, but compared to the average gerbil – I am an intellectual giant.

Take Thermal for instance. When it comes to dribbling a ping pong ball or climbing up the velvet curtains in five seconds flat, then I am no match for him.

But when I decide it is time for him to put his ping pong ball away and he disagrees, I simply tap him on the left shoulder and, as he looks round, I pick up the ball from somewhere near his right front paw and slip it into my pocket. We have been doing this every night since he arrived and he still doesn't know what happens to it.

With humans I have problems. Humans know so many things that I shall never know. They know about cars, how my television works and why my photocopier keeps getting jammed.

Only last Thursday the man from Rank Xerox spent ages explaining to me exactly how my photocopier works so that I wouldn't get it jammed in future.

I didn't understand a word he said. I nodded intelligently at what seemed to be the right moments, but he had left me floundering long ago – up to my knees in status codes.

I try to tell myself that we all have our strengths and our weaknesses. Some of us are technically minded and some of us are not. If the photocopier man had had a ping pong ball with him, I could have whipped it away without his knowing and he would have been ever so impressed. But he hadn't – so I couldn't.

Animals also allow me to make a fool of myself without comment. I often make a fool of myself in front of Thermal and never once has he criticized me or seemed ashamed of me.

We settled down to play 'gas fires'. Maybe you don't play 'gas fires' with your cat, but then that's probably because you don't have a gas fire with a wrought-iron surround.

It's a great game for a cold winter's day because I can sit in front of the fire and wiggle my fingers through the holes, while Thermal crawls underneath and tries to catch my finger as it comes out on the other side.

Tigger went off to do her rounds in the cellar and I would have waved goodbye to her except that I had my finger stuck in a sharp little hole and I couldn't get it out.

Thermal was having a rare old time on the other side and was giving my finger hell, but after a time he began to get bored. It was too easy – usually he wins some and he loses some, winning all the time was no fun at all. He came out to see what was going on.

'I'm sorry, old son – I've got my finger stuck.'

'*Oh dear.*'

He seemed to understand, and he sat by my side and worried about the problem.

I worried as well. My finger had been stuck there for over half an hour now and it was beginning to swell.

'*Does it hurt?*'

'Yes.'

'*Oh dear.*'

I once got my finger stuck in one of those silly holes they have in pan handles – that hurt as well, but at least I was able to walk over to the fridge and smear butter on my finger.

There was no way I was going to be able to walk over to the kitchen with a gas fire stuck on my finger and so Thermal and I wiggled away butterlessly and worried together.

'Butter – fetch!'

'*Pardon?*'

'Never mind.'

To his credit, not once did Thermal say '*You daft devil,*' or '*I've told you before you'd get your finger stuck.*' He just sat there with his brow furrowed and tried very hard to think of a solution.

The fact that he didn't come up with a solution is neither here nor there. I was none too pleased when he burrowed back under the fire and began belting the living daylights out of my finger yet again, but I like to think he was just trying to help – a sort of shock therapy.

'*I was locked in a garage for a month.*'

'Yes I know.'
'Try licking the fireplace.'

I had tried licking my finger but by the time Aileen arrived back I had been stuck there for almost two hours.

'I thought you were supposed to be working?'

That was the first thing she said. When I told her that I had my finger stuck in the fire surround, the second and third things she said were, 'You daft devil,' and 'I've told you before you'd get your finger stuck.'

With humans you always get criticism. I suppose I should add that with humans you also get help. She nipped into the kitchen and came back with a bottle of cooking oil which she proceeded to squirt on my finger.

It took some time to work it free, mainly because Thermal insisted on licking off the oil from the other side, but eventually I was able to jerk it clear and I think we shall stick to the ping pong ball from now on.

Anne and Alex came to dinner that night. So did Thermal. I brought a Chinese in and Thermal loves Chinese. Over the sweet and sour Aileen told them all about my finger and the fire and they laughed their heads off.

Thermal didn't laugh – he just concentrated on his prawn cracker and didn't say a word.

That's what I like about animals. Thermal doesn't expect me to be any brighter than he is, even though he can shin up the trellis faster than I can.

When I come back to this world I think I shall come back as a kitten – I only hope I get an owner who is as daft as I am.

I may have deficiencies as a husband, father and provider. But as a cat owner, soulmate and finger wiggler – I reckon I am just about damn near perfect.

Chapter Eighteen

The day started off a little too early for my liking. It exploded into living colour at just after a quarter past six and several minutes had passed before I was able to adjust my eyeballs sufficiently to make out Thermal playing snooker on the dressing table.

He was trying to pot Aileen's contact lens with her eyebrow pencil. I grabbed him by the scruff of the neck and carted him off downstairs.

'Ouch!'

'Do you know what time I went to bed?'

'Half past two – you woke me up.'

'Half past two.'

'I just said that.'

'And do you know what time it is now?'

'Seventeen minutes past six.'

'It's eighteen minutes past six.'

'That clock's fast.'

'I'm not having it – do you understand?'

'It can be adjusted.'

Tigger opened bleary eyes as we swept past her – she had been fast asleep on the bottom shelf of the tea trolley. As part of her quest for sainthood she seemed to be practising self-mortification and had spent the previous night draped over the toaster.

'What?'

'Go back to sleep – it's all right.'

I opened the back door and planted Thermal on the balcony.

'You can play out there – go on.'

'It's a sheet of ice.'

'No it isn't.'

'Black ice.'

'Push off.'

'I haven't had my boiled egg yet.'

I picked up the three bottles of milk from the step, slipped the milkman's note into the pocket of my robe and shut the door behind me. Sometimes you have to be hard.

I had never met the milkman. He left two green-tops and one red-top at well before six o'clock every morning and at that time, Thermal permitting, I am usually involved in a semi-conscious tug of war with Aileen over possession of the duvet.

He also left me a note every morning. It had all started just before Christmas when I opened the back door and found nine green-top bottles lined up in a row. At the far end, lost and lonely, was a red-top bottle all on its own.

They looked just like the Plymouth Argyle football team – if for statistical purposes, you assume that one green-top bottle had been sent off for swearing and the red-top was the goalkeeper.

I took them in and cleared a space in the fridge. I kept six and found a good home for the other four, and then left a note for the milkman explaining what had happened and that we wouldn't need any more that week.

I can't remember exactly how I put this message down on paper, but the milkman thought it was very funny and left a note for me telling me how much he appreciated my sense of humour.

Most of his customers, he wrote, would have traced him to the ends of the earth and pushed the bottles up somewhere very unpleasant.

The next morning I left him another note telling him that I would never dream of doing such a thing with a pint bottle of milk. A double cream perhaps, but a pint bottle – never. One had to have some standards.

The following day I found a full sheet of A4 paper and on it, in small neat handwriting, were the milkman's thoughts on society today.

Since then we had exchanged notes every morning without fail, and while I was in London I left Aileen a handful to leave out in my absence. These were supposed to have been written by Thermal, who complained that the rattling of crates jerked him out of a deep sleep every morning and if it didn't stop soon, he and a few of his mates were going to duff up the milkman and teach him a lesson he would never forget.

When I got back Aileen had a collection of replies, all addressed to Thermal – challenging him to a duel with green-top bottles at thirty paces.

It had been great fun, but last night I had been struggling with the book and I had business letters to write and there I was, at two o'clock in the morning, struggling to find a fresh idea so that I could write a note to the milkman.

I thought 'This is stupid,' and so I had written 'Two green-tops and one red-top' on a piece of paper and stuck it outside with the week's money on top.

The doorbell jangled, and there was the little old man who had helped rescue Thermal.

'Thought I ought to tell you – your lad's up tree again.'

'Same one?'

'Aye.'

'How does he do it?'

'Beats me.'

For a moment I thought of leaving him there until dusk, but my better nature got the better of me.

'I'll get the ladder.'

'I'll go and arrange them cones.'

I had the ladder under one arm and Thermal under the other as the old man opened the cellar door for me. Arthur shot through the cat-flap in a blind panic as I stowed the ladder away on the wall.

'You're one of them cat lovers I see.'

'No – I'm not really. I just seem to have drifted into it.'

Tigger glared at me for breaking up her early morning prayer meeting and went off to drag Arthur back into the fold. The old man took Thermal from me and examined him closely.

'He looks a bit pale.'

'He's a white cat.'

'Even so.'

Thermal looked as right as rain – I was the one who was white around the gills. The traffic had been heavy this morning and the old man had directed it from the safety of the pavement.

I still couldn't work out how Thermal had got up there and another close examination of the tree had convinced me that it was impossible unless he used a trampoline.

'I've got to go up to the shops this morning.'

'Have you?'

'To the supermarket – for my cigarettes.'

'Right.'

'It's starting to rain.'

'Would you like a lift?'

'Be very nice.'

This was going to be the set price from now on. Free transportation in exchange for his sharp eyes and his cone-management abilities. The thought crossed my mind that he might be the one who was hurling Thermal up the tree.

I took a look around the cellar. Kay and Stuart Evans were coming to stay with us. Kay had been the Deputy Editor of *Woman's Hour* in my early days and Stuart was a proper author like Aileen. They had forsaken the bright lights of London and now lived in Grimsby – the pace of life in Huddersfield might be too much for them.

'Is it all right if we bring the hounds?'

'How many hounds have you got?'

I could imagine dozens of little tails pointing upwards, straight to the sky, as they belted across the fields and through the woods.

'Just the two – Theakstone and Jennings.'

My heart went out to the dogs. Having to live with Kay and Stuart was bad enough without being named after a couple of Yorkshire breweries. All the same, I didn't fancy having Thermal and Tigger torn to pieces by a couple of four-legged lager louts.

This time it was the hounds who would have to go to earth – in the cellar.

As it happens they caught us unawares. All four of us were suffering from duvet deprivation. Thermal was trying out the bottom shelf of the tea trolley for a change and Tigger had moved up a layer. Aileen was fast asleep on the settee and I was curled up on the hearth rug when the doorbell rang.

I heaved open the door and in came Kay and Stuart with Theakstone and Jennings. I couldn't take my eyes off the dogs.

'What on earth are they?'

'They're lovely,' Kay said.

'I'm sure they are – but what sort are they?' They were wire-haired, miniature dachshunds and they *were* lovely. Just six months old and about three inches tall, they were very serious little dogs who obviously did extremely well at school and never caused their teacher a moment's trouble.

'Thermal will kill them,' I thought, and at that moment the two cats strode into the hall. Theakstone and Jennings moved closer to each other until their little flanks were touching. They trembled together in perfect pitch.

'Don't worry,' Kay told them, 'they are only cats.'

'Only,' I thought. Thermal and Tigger stood side by side like the Lone Ranger and Tonto, staring down at the miniature, wire-haired Abbott and Costello.

My mind was racing – perhaps I should have locked the *cats* in the cellar. Then Thermal walked straight up to Theakstone and sniffed at his nose. Theakstone flicked out a tongue and licked his face.

Thermal loved it. He rubbed his head against Theakstone's cheek and then started on Jennings.

Tigger snorted and turned back towards the trolley. *'Doesn't he embarrass you?'*

She joined in later on, however, and I still can't get over the sight of my two cats towering above the two little dachshunds – all four of them charging about the house like kids on a day trip to Blackpool.

That night, before we went to bed, we had to tear them apart and it wasn't easy. All four of them lay in a pile under the sideboard, and as we pulled out first one and then another, they slid back underneath. It was like trying to unravel a cardigan.

Thermal was too busy to wake me the next morning,

there was far too much going on downstairs, but I seemed to be getting a taste for the early hours.

I fed the animals and went straight to work in the office. I put in a good hour before the neighbours began to pull back their curtains and I would have done more if Thermal hadn't decided to demonstrate the finer points of American football to Theakstone and Jennings.

Enough was enough and I led them off down to the cellar where they could charge about to their hearts' content – Arthur must have gone down to the Job Centre. It never occurred to me that Theakstone was small enough to go out through the cat-flap – even if he'd had Jennings strapped to his back.

From my office window I could see Denton, his coal-black fur on red alert as he stalked up the garden path. Tigger would have sniffed at the flowers – Denton seemed to resent them being there at all and slapped a daffodil on the head as a warning to the others.

He had just sharpened his claws on the holly bush when he saw Thermal coming round the corner – on his own. He must have thought it was Christmas all over again. Thermal, without Tigger riding shotgun – it was what he had always wanted.

He dropped flat against the soil, back-end swaying as he wound himself up for the charge. Thermal had stopped now and was looking over his shoulder, back at the courtyard.

Denton went for it, leaves and soil spinning in his wake as he came out from behind the stone mushroom. He went up the path like a rocket and ran slap bang into four vicious bundles of teeth, hair and fur flying straight towards him like the whole Apache nation.

He went back down the path like Steve Cram on heat. He didn't go over the hedge or under it – he went straight through it and over the road and into the park.

Our four heroes shouted rude things after him as they watched him go and then settled down to a raucous session of last one on the mushroom's a cissy.

Denton watched them from across in the park, his face a picture of horror. He would have nightmares for months to come – or was he dreaming now? He could swear that two of those cats were barking.

Chapter Nineteen

The old man had asked me if I was 'one of them cat lovers' and I had more or less denied it. I had never thought of myself as a cat lover. I liked cats – but then I like dogs and rabbits and gerbils. I once visited Belle Vue Zoo three times in a week just to see a water buffalo.

If an animal will meet me halfway then I am putty in its paws or in its hoofs or whatever, but the old man had me labelled along with those women in the television commercials who babble on breathlessly about what their little Fifi will or will not eat and I didn't like that at all.

So what the hell was I doing walking back from the garage at six thirty in the morning with a tin of Whiskas for Arthur's breakfast?

Thermal and Tigger had shared a coley fillet, microwaved to perfection in two minutes flat. But Arthur didn't like fish, and so here I was, out in a thin drizzle at the crack of dawn, with a tin of beef and kidney in my hand.

When Arthur had first limped down to the cellar he had eaten everything I put before him and then had a go at the pattern on the saucer. But a soft bed and a full stomach turns the gobbler into a gourmet and any day now he would be complaining because I hadn't chilled his white wine properly.

I didn't really mind, the fresh air was more than welcome. I had just worked right through the night and there were seven freshly printed pages lying on my desk.

There was a bounce in my step as I turned into the lane and saw my faithful cat Thermal waiting for me. He had wanted to come with me, across the busy main road to the garage.

'No.'

He had stopped.

'Sit.'

He sat.

'Wait.'

He had waited for me.

'Good boy – come on.'

He came, trotting alongside me, back down the lane like a best of breed at Crufts. He really was a most intelligent cat. I must spend more time training him, he was maturing now and who knows what we could achieve together.

He jumped up on the wall.

'Come down.'

He sat and stared at me as I patted my thigh.

'Heel.'

He glared at me and then turned his attention to the enormous Alsatian who had been following us along the lane, and who was now under the impression that I meant him.

I turned and wagged my finger at Thermal.

'Stay.'

He stood up, had a long low stretch and then looked over his shoulder at me as he sauntered off along the wall.

'*Prat.*'

The Alsatian was now sitting on my left foot and eagerly awaiting my next command.

'Go home.'

He didn't know that one.

'Push off.'

He didn't know that one either, but my tone seemed to offend him and he growled.

'Nice doggy.'

He wasn't going anywhere – he had his eye on the tin of cat food. He growled again, this time in a lower register, a bit like Al Pacino, and fastened his jaws around the tin.

My fingers were also around the tin, so I let him have it and he padded off back down the lane – I had been mugged within a hundred yards of my own house.

I would have followed him, wrestled him to the ground and torn the tin from between his slavering jaws, but I had a bit of a headache coming on – and then my attention was diverted by the sight of a large van reversing off the waste ground.

It stopped for a moment outside my back gate, so that the driver could kick the cold engine back to life and sort out one of his forward gears.

Thermal seemed to have been waiting for it. He stepped off the wall and sat down on the roof of the cab with all the *savoir-faire* of a kitten who has been commuting for years. If he'd had his briefcase with him he would have been sorting through his papers by the time the van moved off, very slowly, coughing and spitting down the lane.

I reacted instantaneously. In a flash my mouth fell wide open and I slipped swiftly into a catatonic trance.

The van bounced round the end of the lane with Thermal still glued to the cab roof like Lester Piggott, hanging on with his claws clamped fast and his bum clenched tight.

It was heading for Park Drive – if it turned left it would be lost for ever, if it turned right it would come up past the front of the house.

I leapt into action. My lithe body hurling itself through the gate and down the steps. Powerful legs took me sailing across the courtyard and down the path. Tigger stepped out of the bushes. *'Arthur says he hasn't had . . .'*

'In a minute.'

I hurtled past her and on towards the front garden. Arthur hurtled past me, his arthritis forgotten for the moment.

'I haven't had my . . .'

'For God's sake – not now.'

The van had turned right and was poddling up the road towards the house. At first I thought Thermal must have fallen off, I couldn't see him on the roof.

But then his head popped up and for a brief moment he rested his chin on a sign that read, 'Fresh Fruit Daily', before ducking back down again, content that the driver was following his instructions to the letter.

I had just nipped down the steps and was about to open the gate when I pulled the muscle in my thigh. My body wasn't used to being lithe and my legs were only powerful over a measured distance of three yards.

God it hurt. Arthur knew how I felt – he seemed to have pulled his entire body and was lying semi-conscious under the hedge.

I had to stop the van. I limped out to the road, but Thermal's second-in-command had already brought it to a halt opposite the park and was now striding across the road towards the houses.

It took some of the urgency out of the situation, and I hobbled gingerly along the pavement so that I would be there when he came out again.

Then I stopped and watched as Thermal stood up and walked to the rear of the van like a captain on the bridge. He had a quick sniff at an interesting rivet and then, with the casual confidence of a kitten who could have done this in his sleep, he hopped a couple of feet up in the air and landed safely on the overhanging branch of the unclimbable tree.

Tigger was waiting for me as I pushed open the gate. Whatever the pantomime going on around her she always remained calm and dignified. She never broke into a sweat like the rest of us.

'I was trying to tell you . . .'

'Yes I know – Arthur hasn't had his breakfast.'

'He's weak from hunger and his legs have gone.'

I scooped him up from under the hedge and carried

him. It was the first time he had ever let me touch him – the first time he hadn't been able to hide behind the central-heating boiler in the cellar until Tigger told him that dinner was served and it was safe to come out now.

He lay in my arms, so stiff with terror and arthritis that he would have cracked if I had dropped him.

'Come on Arthur. I think there's a pork chop you might fancy – then you can give me a hand with the ladder.'

I wasn't in too much of a hurry to rescue Thermal. I thought I'd let him stew up there on his branch for a while, until the novelty wore off and the cold and damp told him that there must be a better way of spending the morning.

Arthur enjoyed his pork chop, sucking it into submission and only bringing his tooth into play for the crackly bits. I could hear him dragging it round the kitchen floor as I sat in my office and tried to work.

But my mind wasn't on the job. I worried that Thermal might fall off his branch or step down on to the roof of a passing double-decker and finish up in Holmfirth.

I could only take about half an hour of it and then I hauled the ladder up from the cellar once more, donned my suit of shining armour, and went out to rescue a small cat who would by now be paralysed with fear.

He was having a ball. Joggers were waving to him from the park and pointing him out to the pensioners resting their weary bones on the benches. Lorry drivers, having a late breakfast, put aside their *Daily Mirrors* and tried to tempt him down with bacon butties and beefburgers.

He was showing off something rotten. For their benefit he put on an astonishing display of aerobics and acrobatics, twig twirling and leaping up for leaves. Then he capped it off with a demonstration of branch balancing that had them with their hearts in their mouths.

I wondered if Thermal could do one of those backflips that always leave me wondering why that twelve-year-old gymnast on the beam didn't break her back when she was seven years old and only practising.

He got a loud cheer as I grabbed him and carried him down the ladder and another round of applause as I carted him across to the house. He leaned over my shoulder and acknowledged the tribute.

'*I'll be back – same time tomorrow.*'

'Oh no you won't.'

That evening I kept an eye open for the fruit van and sure enough, around six o'clock, it chugged back up the lane and came to a halt alongside the wall.

I nipped down the steps and out through the gate. The driver was trying to bend it in between a couple of parked cars on the waste ground – it was the sort of van that took some persuading.

The driver locked the battered door and stood back to admire the view. They looked a pair this man and his van. I half expected him to clip a nosebag on the bonnet and leave it a carrot for afterwards.

'Can I have a word with you?'

'Course you can.'

He had an air of resignation about him, a highly developed sense of forbearance which was something else he shared with the van. He was waiting for me to say, 'You're not going to park that thing there, are you?'

I told him about Thermal pinching free rides on his roof and he relaxed.

'Oh we can't have that, can we. I've seen him around – he's a nice little chap. I'll keep an eye open for him and send him packing.'

We talked about the fruit business – apparently it's not what it was – and then he said, 'The milkman was asking about you this morning. He wanted to know if you were ill or anything. He said you hadn't left him a note.'

I told him that I couldn't spare the time any more.

'I'm spending as much time writing the notes for the milkman as I am on the book.'

He understood perfectly, but he thought it was a shame.

'You know he lost his wife just before Christmas? He says it was only getting your notes and thinking up replies that's got him through these last few months.'

As I walked back to the house I felt as though I had just been hit over the head with two green-tops and a red-top. I collected Thermal from the airing cupboard and together we worked on tomorrow's note.

Sorry, but I've been ill – normal service has

now been resumed and I must take you to task over a very serious matter.

Thermal has brought to my attention the fact that yesterday you did spitefully, and without provocation on Thermal's part, kick his ping pong ball under the garden shed so that it was well out of the reach of an individual with such short paws.

If this sort of behaviour continues, Thermal hereby gives notice that he will consult his solicitor on the matter and you would well be warned that Thermal's solicitor is much bigger than you are.

Thermal's solicitor has a black belt at karate, a green belt at judo and two pairs of extremely smart red and blue braces in a sort of paisley design.

Thermal's solicitor specializes in dealing with stroppy milkmen who terrorize small cats, he has made a career out of it and has a list of successes as long as your arm. You would be well advised to settle out of Court.

The aforementioned Thermal has indicated that he is willing to accept your word in writing as to your future conduct and will accept a small carton of double cream in lieu of damages.

Would you also note that the ping pong ball is not now the same shape as it was before you kicked it under the shed – it is now a square ping pong ball. However, since it is much more fun that way, we do not intend to make an issue of this.

Signed – Thermal Longden in the presence of his owner.

I read it over a couple of times and Thermal checked the spelling.

'What a load of old rubbish,' I thought as I put it out with the milk bottles. But then, you never know just how important a load of old rubbish can be – do you?

Chapter Twenty

Arthur sat just inside the hall doorway. Apart from the one pork chop in the kitchen when his legs had gone it was as far as he ever ventured into the house. He had often been invited to sit by the fire, but he always refused.

He was a cellar cat, as had been his father before him and *his* father before *him*, and he just popped upstairs every now and then to borrow a saucer of milk or to ask us if we would kindly keep the noise down.

Thermal and Tigger sat either side of the suitcase on the Chinese rug and looked as though the world were coming to an end.

'They'll be as right as rain once they're there,' Aileen told me, but she couldn't see those eyes that were accusing me of everything from simple neglect to genocide.

Arthur stood up and, with as much dignity as he could muster, made his position on the matter quite clear. *'Well I'm going nowhere.'* He was filling out, was Arthur. His bald spots were covered with a precarious fluff and the more established fur had taken on a healthy sheen. For all that, he still looked like a badly stuffed night-dress case and his dignity made you smile.

Bridie was going to look after Arthur. His needs were few, just a drop of milk, a kind word every now and then and a shovelful of Whiskas twice a day. He would toast himself by the boiler in his cellar over the long weekend, but the rest of the house was wired up with a series of burglar alarms that would have taken Bridie a month to work out.

We put the bags in the boot and the cats in the car and set off for the five star Cat-Motel of which we had heard good things.

I don't know quite what I had expected. A single room perhaps, with en suite shower, a colour television and full use of the cruet.

Looking back I suppose it was a bit much to expect all that for £1.75 a day and the accommodation turned out to be a couple of small apartments in a sort of high-rise rabbit hutch.

There was a double-sided feeding bowl with a portion of dry mince in one half and water in the other. Tigger hadn't touched water since she was a kitten and she'd be damned if she was starting now.

Thermal was appalled. His floor was lined with newspaper – the *Independent* dated 23 February. He'd read it and he was not at all pleased.

Mrs Kaufman tipped the balance. She seemed a kindly old soul and her cardigan was covered with so many cat hairs that you could have stuffed Arthur all over again. She must give them the odd cuddle.

'We let them have a run twice a day,' she told us, and the two cats looked at one another. I knew what they were thinking – a tunnel, that's what they were thinking.

But their eyes had lost that momentary glow by the time we turned to leave. '*How could you?*' they said, and I felt like something that had just crawled out from under a stone.

They wouldn't have let them into the Savoy Hotel. They wouldn't let me in – not to the Women of the Year Luncheon anyway, and Aileen was spirited from my side the moment we set foot in the River Room entrance.

I hovered on a small landing, waiting to catch a glimpse of her as she was escorted up the main stairway to be presented to the Duchess of Kent.

I hung around for a while, but then my little landing began to fill with luncheon guests who had taken a wrong turning through the hotel and who were now queuing up to squeeze through the narrow doorway.

I made my excuses and left, cutting through the hotel towards the main entrance. A door burst open and a familiar face, looking all flustered, flew out of a room marked Private.

'Excuse me, love,' said Su Pollard, 'have you any idea where this women's do is?'

'Yes – I've just come from there.'

'Would you take me, only I keep getting lost.'

I tried to steer her back towards the landing, but I lost her twice within a hundred yards and had to go looking for her again, and so I took a firm hold of her hand to make sure we both went the same way.

She was wearing a wondrous outfit and she was probably the only woman in the whole wide world it would have suited.

'Do you work here?'

'No – my wife's at the luncheon.'

'That's where I'm going.'

After a few false starts I made it back to the landing. It was empty now, but a guard stood on duty at the door. She put her arm out and stopped us.

'You can't come in here.'

'Not me – just the lady.'

She turned to Su and seemed to assume she was wearing some African national costume. She spoke loudly and clearly so that the actress would understand.

'Have you got an invitation?'

'Yes, love – it's on the sideboard at home.'

'What about a badge?'

'It's on the sideboard – with my invitation.'

'Then I'm very sorry.'

'Can't you make an exception this once, only I think I'm quite famous.'

She couldn't, and we stood there on tiptoe for a while, watching the passing parade through a curtain of swinging earrings and a solid mass of shoulder pads. I whispered to my newfound friend.

'I wish I was six foot four – I should be able to see my wife then.'

She thought that was terrible – that I couldn't see my wife.

'Here, love,' she cried, 'you can sit on my shoulders if you like,' and she bent down double so that I could climb aboard.

I didn't though. I just watched the top of Aileen's head as it talked to the top of the Duchess of Kent's head and then drifted off once more. They let Su Pollard in before I left.

'She's from *Hi-De-Hi*,' a companion told the guard.

The guard nodded. Geography wasn't her strong point, but judging from the costume, she'd guessed it would be somewhere exotic.

I wandered round Covent Garden for a while with a beef sandwich in one hand and a carton of sweet tea in the other, but soon it was time to make tracks back to the Savoy.

I had arranged to watch the speeches on a BBC television monitor in the press room and I sat down behind a row of reporters. The camera zoomed in on Aileen as she struggled with her Pear Belle Helene.

She chased it round her plate but it was a tricky little devil and it wasn't giving up easily. She gave it a thwack with her spoon, stunning it, and then dug in deep while the pear was still wondering what had happened. The spoon came up empty, but she sucked it anyway.

'I liked her,' said a reporter, 'she was nice.'

'The writer?' asked her companion.

'Yes – I hope she wins.'

'So do I.'

I leaned forward. I wanted to give them both a kiss, but I didn't.

'She's mine,' I told them, as Aileen frowned in close-up and then went after the pear again. A hand, holding a fork, appeared in the bottom left hand corner of the screen and waited until the pear came round once more. Then it moved in, like lightning, pinning it to the plate.

Aileen smiled at her off-screen benefactor and then quickly disembowelled her pudding.

'We'll keep our fingers crossed,' the reporters said.

She was still fizzing with champagne the next morning as we turned off the motorway towards the Cat-Motel. A *Daily Telegraph* lay on the back seat of the car, open at page four with its large photograph of Aileen and the headline, 'Blind novelist is Woman of the Year.'

We had talked non-stop all the way from London and we hadn't finished yet. Aileen floated about an inch above the passenger seat and wore a smile that had oncoming drivers swerving out of the way.

'The Duchess said she was a reader of mine.'

'Good for her.'

'She said she liked my shirt.'

'It's a nice shirt.'

'I hope the cats are all right.'

'Did she say that?'

'No I did.'

'To the Duchess?'

'No – just now.'

They weren't all right. They were decidedly not all right and they didn't hesitate to let us know about it.

'They've been very naughty,' Mrs Kaufman told us, and Thermal scowled.

'She threatened me.'

'He pushed all his food out through the bars.'

'Best place for it.'

'He scratched me on the arm.'

'I think I've got blood poisoning.'

'Next time you leave them here I shall . . .'

But there wasn't going to be a next time. When I had to leave them again it would be at home with Bridie to look after them. I had three months to teach her how to handle the burglar alarm – Aileen could teach me and then I would teach Bridie.

Arthur had had a wonderful time. He'd hardly moved from his boiler – he'd eaten seconds and thirds and fourths and fifths, so Bridie told us, and he looked as though he might explode any minute.

Thermal was so excited to be home that he forgot to be miserable and the moment he laid eyes on his sultana he went berserk. They clattered around the house together, Thermal like a small pit pony, the sultana like a small pit pony's tame sultana, and they toured all their favourite window-sills, upstairs and downstairs, until they were exhausted. Then they sat on the fax machine and warmed their bums.

I put some fish in the microwave oven and on the second ping they were both in the kitchen, the sultana somewhat unwillingly – he never felt comfortable in the kitchen. He had been told as a child of the great Eccles cake massacre of '87 in which most of his family had been wiped out.

He never spoke about it, but I believe a mixing bowl and an egg whisk were supposed to have been involved. It was all a bit hazy now – he was no more than a currant at the time.

Tigger wouldn't eat, she wouldn't do anything. She just sat under Aileen's desk with her back to us and made us suffer. She wasn't sulking – she was hurt, and she couldn't understand how we could have put her in that terrible place. I tried my best.

'Come on, love – come and have something to eat.'

Her head turned slowly and her eyes met mine. There was a simple depth to them, more eloquent than any words, and they told me that she needed time to think about this – if I wouldn't mind.

Patrick rang and invited us round. He and Sarah had watched Aileen on the television and they wanted to celebrate with a drink.

We celebrated with one and then another and then several more as the evening went on. Aileen knocked over her usual glass quite early in the proceedings and so I was able to relax and enjoy myself. She always breaks one glass, but I've never known her break two.

We got up to leave in the early hours and as Patrick opened the door into the porch there was a clattering noise.

'What was that?' Aileen asked.

'The cat-flap,' Patrick told her.

'Cat-flap? I didn't know you had a cat?'

'We haven't,' said Patrick, glancing at me as he stood back to let us through. 'But we did have – if you remember.'

Tigger was still under Aileen's desk when I looked in on her – she hadn't finished thinking about it yet and I left her to it. I just hoped that it wouldn't be too long.

As Aileen pushed open the bedroom door I could see Thermal flat out on the duvet. I decided to tackle him right away.

'You never told me you had a cat-flap.'

He was obviously too embarrassed to answer.

'When you were little – you could have gone indoors.'

He continued to ignore me.

'You were putting it on, weren't you?'

He snored – he was fast asleep and I decided to leave it for now and have it out with him over breakfast.

It must have been somewhere around five o'clock in the morning when I experienced that strange sensation that tells you a cat is walking up the entire length of your body.

The sensation nuzzled my cheek and then shimmied down inside the duvet, tucking itself into the crook of my arm. I could feel a warm naked bottom from Aileen's side of the bed and a warm furry body up against my chest.

I moved my legs slightly and there was Thermal's sturdy weight, still lying heavily across my feet.

Then a muffled purr ruffled the single hair on my chest and I smiled to myself – it looked as though Tigger had thought it over and I was forgiven.

Chapter Twenty-One

Thermal and Tigger were charging round the court-yard, playing one and a half-a-side football with Chico – it's a version of the game you don't see all that often these days.

Arthur was sitting on the balcony, proudly sham-pooing the nervous black fluff that sprouted from his legs and chest. I can't be absolutely sure, but I could swear that before he started to sprout he had the words 'Mother' tattooed on one paw and 'Millwall' on the other.

He was a very contented cat, and he liked to sit up there and preen himself as his former fellow travellers snuffled around the dustbins below.

'I told you I'd make it one day – this is my place now, so push off.'

Bridie sat on the bottom step with me, coaching Chico from the sideline. He had a natural talent for the game, spiced with just a touch of Irish individuality – his ball control was exceptional and time and time again he burst through the opposing defence only to be flattened at the last minute.

'That wasn't fair, Thermal.'

'Worked though, didn't it?'

★   ★   ★

Only a few minutes earlier I had been an integral part of a BBC television crew who were up in Aileen's study filming an interview.

There was a producer, an interviewer, a cameraman and a lighting man, a sound engineer, the producer's assistant and me, all of us working together as a team.

'Who'd like a cup of tea?'

'Two sugars please – no milk.'

'No sugar and just a drop of milk.'

'Very weak, lots of milk and no sugar.'

'Do you have lemon?'

'Coffee please, sweeteners if you have them and very little milk – just show it the jug.'

And I'd got every one right. I couldn't remember which one was whose, but they sorted it out eventually and their grimaces faded as the original order hit the spot. A television crew marches on its bladder and I felt there might be an opening for me here.

But Thermal blew my big chance of a move into the media. He chased into the room after a trailing cable and was thrilled to see such a crowd.

He loves nothing better than a party, he's your 'life and soul' type of cat and he leapt up on to Aileen's knee to find out what was going on. The interviewer ploughed on regardless. 'With your sight problem – how do you manage to research your novels?'

'Well – I . . .'

Aileen tried to finish the sentence, but Thermal had just spotted the tiny microphone she had so enjoyed having threaded up the inside of her dress and clipped to her lapel.

'That shouldn't be there.'

First he stunned it with a right cross and before it knew where it was he had the little button clamped between his teeth. Then he saw the wire disappearing between Aileen's breasts and decided to go down after it and sort it out once and for all.

The sound man's eyeballs were revolving at a rate of knots as he ripped off his headphones. The producer leapt forward and went down Aileen's dress after the cat.

It was some time before normal service was resumed, and then the producer showed his growing faith in my talents by appointing me to the post of official cat-controller in addition to my already onerous duties as tea-boy.

'I'm sorry about that . . .' Aileen began.

'Was I all right?'

'Shut up,' I muttered.

'Did they get my best side?'

'Sit still.'

'. . . only Thermal often sits on my desk and watches me type.'

'That's not a bad idea,' the producer mused, 'let's give it a try.'

They should have known from his earlier performance that Thermal wasn't born to be an extra.

He sat for a moment or two watching Aileen's fingers as they flew across the keyboard, but then, as she turned to explain a point, he marched across it himself – stamping words in pure Hungarian up on the screen.

Safely over on the other side, he leaned his chin on Aileen's shoulder and grinned at the camera.

'Right – let's have him out.'

He was handed to the official cat-controller, who was now in fear of losing his job.

'Would you all like a nice cup of tea?'

'No thank you – just get rid of him.'

They had shut the study door behind me and there was no way I could get back in – I might disturb the sound balance and they had had enough of that for one day, and so I had found myself carrying the child prodigy down to the courtyard where Bridie waited for me with Chico tucked under her arm.

'Listen to this.'

We all three of us stared at Chico, waiting to hear what he had to say.

'Come on, Chico.'

Chico is the strong silent type, which is most unusual for an Irishman and even more unusual for an O'Connell.

'Come on.'

Bridie poked him in the ribs and he complained bitterly in a raw throaty squawk.

'There,' she said, 'do you think his voice is breaking?'

The football match had to be abandoned when the postman walked across the pitch and the players bolted.

I held out my hand for the letters he was holding out in front of him, but he had his head down as usual

and he walked straight
past me and began to
climb the steps.

Arthur panicked and
came hobbling down,
Thermal flew past
him on the way up
and Tigger and
Chico went off with
Bridie to discuss tactics.

He wasn't the fastest postman in Huddersfield.
It was now almost lunch-time and if he tackled his
round as he tackled the steps it was a wonder he ever
got here at all.

As he rammed a handful through the letterbox,
I said, 'Excuse me please,' and walked past him and
picked them off the mat. The door was wide open
now, but he still pushed the next bunch through the
letterbox and I had to remove a couple of them from
the pocket of an overcoat that was hanging on a hook.

'How much longer is this going on?' he demanded.

'Is what going on?'

'These letters – and these.'

He produced several Jiffy bags and a parcel.

'This is the last call on my round. I've had to
haul this lot every inch of the way – it's been a week
now.'

The producer's assistant tapped me on the shoulder.

'Any chance of another cup of tea?'

I'd got my job back – there was still time to
make an impression.

'Right away.' I turned to the postman. 'Would you like a cup?'

'No thanks – I live across the park.'

'What's that got to do with anything?' the girl asked him. 'Don't they drink tea over there?'

'No, it's not that,' he handed me the Jiffy bags, 'it's just that my wife will be watching me through the binoculars.'

The producer's assistant and I zoomed our eyeballs across the park.

'She watches you – through binoculars?'

'Oh aye. If I went into a house for a cup of tea with a lady, she'd play merry England.'

I was just about to point out, just in case he hadn't noticed, that I wasn't a lady when he leaned forward and asked the assistant, 'Excuse me, love – would you do me a favour?'

'If I can,' she said.

He shuffled to one side and pointed to a gap between the trees.

'I live over there. Would you come out on the balcony and wave across the park?'

'What for?'

'I'd appreciate it – and so would the wife.'

'Anything for a quiet life,' she said, stepping out through the doorway and hoisting a self-conscious arm into the air. 'That all right?'

'Just once more for good measure. She might not have got the first one.'

She gave another wave to the unseen enemy and then, as she turned, she saw Thermal sitting on the roof.

'How did he get up there?'

It does look rather dramatic when you first see a cat sitting on a chimney, four storeys above the ground. It's even more riveting to watch him pick his way along the guttering, paws on points like Margot Fonteyn.

He can work his way right round the house in the guttering, and I had often wondered, just to be on the safe side, if I should get him one of those balancing poles that The Great Houdini used to carry.

'It's quite simple really,' I explained. 'He jumps from the bed to the dressing table and then on to the wardrobe and goes out through the Velux window in the roof. He frightens the life out of the birds – they don't expect an attack from behind when they're having forty winks.'

She stared at Thermal in wonder as I talked and he caught her eye, went all embarrassed and began to do his silly walk along the ridge tiles.

The postman had his eye on the girl, and as she disappeared back in the house he tapped me on the shoulder and whispered, 'How could she see the cat?'

'Well he's up there – look.'

'But she's supposed to be blind.'

'No – Aileen's supposed to be blind. That was a lady from the BBC.'

It took a little while for this to sink in and then he turned and gestured across the park with a wild, ship-to-shore, sort of a wave.

'That wasn't her,' he shouted. 'That was a woman

from the BBC. I'll get the other one in a minute.'

He turned back to me. 'She'll be quite excited,' he said, 'she watches BBC.'

Just then Aileen came to the door with the interviewer and began to point out interesting backdrops for the next session.

'This is her,' the postman roared, pointing his finger at the interviewer's head. 'This is the Woman of the Year.'

'No it isn't,' I shouted to the space across the park. I poked a finger into Aileen's right ear. 'This is her.'

'What's happening?' Aileen asked.

'Never mind,' I said. 'Just wave across the park and we can all go in and have a cup of tea.'

So she waved – a good long wave with a nice bright smile on her face and then she turned back to me.

'Why did I do that?'

'I'll tell you later – it's a bit like being the Queen.'

I walked down the steps with the postman. He'd got rid of his letters, but he seemed to have all the cares of the world on his shoulders.

'I'll have to get a move on,' he said. 'She times me – she watches me walk across the park and she gets annoyed if I stop and talk to anyone.'

I began to wish we hadn't bothered waving to this crabby old woman who watched the world and her husband through a pair of binoculars, and then I had an awful feeling that I might be misjudging her – she might be disabled and this was her only way of keeping in touch.

221

'Is she disabled?' I asked him. 'Can't she get about?'

'Oh aye,' he said, 'she can get about. It's just that she's a nosey old devil and she doesn't like to miss anything.'

That afternoon Aileen entertained a reporter from the *Yorkshire Post*, another film crew, this time from Yorkshire Television, and a free-lance journalist from *Woman's Weekly*.

I granted an audience to a small man with bad breath who had come especially to see me and wanted to talk about patio doors and double glazing.

It was nice to be wanted, but even nicer, when they had all gone, to be able to put our feet up and relax.

'Have you fed the cats?'

'Oh hell.'

I put my feet down and limped out to the kitchen – it was almost an hour after feeding time and I was surprised Thermal hadn't come looking for me.

Tigger never would. She seemed conscious of the fact that she never did any of the cooking or contributed to the upkeep of the household in any way, and she would rather go hungry than have it look as though she were after a hand-out.

Arthur was going through a funny phase. He had landed on his feet and had become as cocky a cat as you ever saw, except during the half-hour leading up to a meal-time – then he seemed to think that it was all too good to last and was a nervous wreck by the time I pushed a saucer under his nose.

But Thermal had no such qualms. He knew his

rights, and he also knew when it was six o'clock on the button, so where on earth was he?

Then I remembered. He wasn't on earth at all – he was up on the roof and I'd forgotten all about him. He could get down on his own, but the window had a habit of slamming shut.

Due to a certain deficiency in the back leg area I am not as nimble as Thermal, and the leap from the dressing table to the wardrobe is a bit too much for me. So I hauled a pair of steps up from cellar to bedroom and stuck them under the window.

It had snapped shut and I half expected to see an angry young cat glaring in at me from the other side, tapping his wristwatch in frustration.

But there was no cat – at least, not on the flat roof that surrounds the dome, nor on the tiles that climb towards the two chimneys.

I shouted, and a row of damp pigeons took off into the night – all except the deaf one at the far end.

They must have been very brave or extremely stupid to settle down with Thermal on the prowl and they didn't look either – except for the deaf one at the far end who looked very stupid indeed.

For a man who suffers panic attacks on the third rung of a ladder, the next five minutes were very painful. I clambered up the wet tiles to all four ridges and peered down at the guttering on the other side. I even had a peep down one of the chimneys, but there was no sign of Thermal – it was just me and the pigeon.

The courtyard was about the size of a dining table from up there, the paving slabs glistened and looked very hard.

There was a cat lying flat on its stomach by the edge of the steps – it was Chico, and he seemed disturbed by something he had just discovered in the flower bed.

I had better go down and have a look. I just hoped it wasn't what I thought it was.

Chapter Twenty-Two

It wasn't Thermal – it was Denton. He was hugging the ground like a sniper, lying half submerged amongst the Azalea Japonica.

He wouldn't have known what they were called, of course, he couldn't read the words on the little stick. But he did know that Chico couldn't see him properly from over there, and was coming over here to have a closer look.

Denton licked his lips in anticipation. This was just the way to keep in trim after a night out with the lads – taking a big lump out of Chico.

And then this ugly great bloke who doesn't know the first thing about the law of the jungle comes blundering in and treads on your tail. It's just not fair – it plays hell with your nerves and it doesn't do your tail much good either.

It was the first time I had ever been pleased to see Denton, and if he had stayed around long enough for me to say thank you I would have kissed him. That sinking feeling in the pit of my stomach

had told me that I was going to find a badly battered Thermal lying there in the flower bed.

But the relief soon rolled over into anxiety, and with the faithful Chico acting as my chief scout I worked my way around the edges of the house, hoping against hope that we wouldn't find anything.

We didn't, and Chico seemed to think he had let me down – but then he didn't know what we were looking for.

I searched the roof once more that night and then again in the morning, but there was no trace of him and I wondered if he could have fallen down the chimney and be boarded up behind one of the gasfires . . .

'It's not like him,' Aileen told me. 'He's very surefooted.'

'I know he is.'

'You worry too much.'

'I know I do.'

'He's probably got a girlfriend somewhere.'

'Yes, I suppose you're right.'

The man from North Eastern Gas arrived spot on twelve o'clock and removed first one gasfire and then the other. He found a very stiff thrush and a small piece of mortar.

'He's probably got a girlfriend somewhere,' he said as he pushed the fire back into place.

'Yes,' I agreed, trying to convince myself that I wasn't actually holding a dead thrush between forefinger and thumb. 'I suppose you're right.'

But Thermal wasn't really interested in girls – the vet had seen to that – and so I punched up the old circular on the Amstrad and, after substituting the words 'half-grown cat' for 'small kitten', I ran off another 150 copies and started on my rounds.

I knew where all the letterboxes were this time, and Tigger came with me to keep me company, walking on the walls where she smelled dogs and danger, trotting up the paths when she sensed that all was well.

She hadn't been able to settle since Thermal disappeared and she followed me around the house like a new puppy. Even Arthur, who possesses all the subtle sensitivity of a half-brick, seemed to notice that something was wrong.

'I could always move in you know – make up the numbers.'

'It's a bit early for that, Arthur.'

'Just thought I'd mention it.'

Two days stretched into four and then the fifth day was a Friday. The woman rang up again about men going round in a van stealing 'em. She must live close by – she had answered the small ad in the *Examiner* last time. I cut her off in her prime and then the doorbell rang. The man had my circular in his hand.

'This yours?'

'Yes.'

'I'm doing up some flats down the road. My men say there's a cat in the building somewhere – been there for a few days, they've heard it, but they haven't seen it.'

'I'll come with you.'

'Bring a torch – the electric isn't on.'

We walked down together to the lovely old house opposite the park. It was so obviously empty that I had hesitated about tackling the drive and the letterbox with my leaflets. Only the work ethic that nags away at me twenty-four hours a day had made me do the job properly.

'He must have come in while we had a window out – we've done it up now and he's stuck.'

I shouted and whistled over the first two floors, but the empty house wasn't at all impressed.

'Come on – we've got two more yet.'

We climbed a staircase that had known better days and I shone my torch over a stack of old floorboards.

'We're replacing 'em.'

I thought I heard something and so did he. We stood still, silent for a time, and then I shouted.

'Thermal!'

'Thermal?'

'That's his name – it's a long story.'

'It must be. I can't be doing with cats myself – I like dogs.'

We climbed to the fourth floor and the torch began to feel the strain. The beam dripped out of the business end and fell to the floor with a limp wrist.

'What sort have you got?'

'A wire-haired terrier?'

'What do you call him?'

'Dinky.'

'Dinky?'

'Yes – well, it's the wife's really.'

The top floor crouched under low beams and didn't seem quite so hollow as the rest of the house. A couple of rooflights came to the assistance of my torch as it attempted a weary search of the far corners.

'He must be up here. My blokes have tried to coax him out, but he wouldn't have nothing to do with them. Just pinched the fillings out of their sandwiches when they weren't looking.'

'That sounds like him – Thermal!' I shouted.

There was a scuttling sound and then nothing.

'Thermal!'

He came like a train under the floorboards, right from over by the gas meter. I could hear him pounding, out of sight, and then he leapt up through the gap between two joists and hit me full in the chest, his claws grabbing at my sweater.

'So that's Thermal.'

'This is him.'

'Mucky little devil,
isn't he?'

His ears went back and
his eyes went wild at the
sound of a stranger's
voice. He struggled to get
away and I had to pin him under
one arm to hold on to him.

'He's a lucky little devil

as well. That's the last floorboard – the electricians would have had it screwed down in the morning.'

The three of us stood in the kitchen and grinned daft grins at one another as Thermal tucked into a large green tin of rabbit and chicken in jelly, and then, as a special treat, a much smaller, tin-coloured tin of silver sardines in olive oil.

He paused for a burp – not one of Tigger's timid bicarbonate burps, delicately masked with a pretty little smile – but a real building-site belch that made the fur round his haunches fold and pucker up into a one inch ruff.

The ruff travelled the entire length of his body, taking up the slack before running out of steam somewhere around the back of his neck and then washing itself out, down over his face.

I could only guess at the sort of language he must have picked up from under the floorboards.

'Pardon me.'

Tigger wrinkled her nose in disgust.

'I should think so.'

'I was hungry – I haven't eaten for a week.'

'You pinched the fillings out of the men's sandwiches,' I reminded him and he winced at the thought.

'Have you ever tried cheese and tomato with Branston pickle?'

It was good to have him back again, and as a nightcap he had the top off the milk almost down to the bottom, before following us upstairs and burying himself under the duvet.

He was fast asleep before I had whipped my shirt off and he had picked his favourite spot – right where I like to tuck my knees up after I've kissed Aileen good night.

I threaded my feet down the bed until my toes touched warm fur and then my legs forked out left and right, sliding either side of him until I was just one digit short of advertising the Isle of Man.

I swivelled my hips, tucked my right arm under my chest and turned over slowly with my left knee in mid-air so as not to disturb him. It was ever so comfortable for the first thirty seconds and then my shoulder froze and went to sleep.

It was the only bit of me that did go to sleep and I was still awake when Tigger jumped on my head.

'*Sorry.*'

She liked to check everything before she came up – to make sure the lights were out and the doors were locked – and then spend a few quiet moments alone on the litter-tray without prying eyes or coarse remarks from Thermal.

'*What is it – arthritis?*'

'No – I've got Thermal between my legs.'

'*So that's where he is – I'll pop down and say good night.*'

She tunnelled under the duvet to join him, and Aileen stirred and turned towards me, just as Thermal stretched his paws and claws at the pleasure of having company.

Aileen's silky whisper brushed my ear.

'Are you awake?'

'Yes,' I told her in a soaring falsetto that brought

231

back memories of the church choir and my first sur-
plice.

'I'm not tired – are you?'

'No.'

'Then why don't we . . .'

'Not just now, love – I think I've got one of
my headaches coming on.'

Arthur came up to see me the next morning. He didn't
have an appointment but I suppose he thought he knew
me well enough. He'd never been in my office before
and so he just popped his head round the door.

'I see he's come back.'

'Yes.'

'So there won't be no vacancy then.'

'What's wrong with the cellar?'

*'Nothing – what's wrong with wanting to go up in
the world?'*

'Nothing.'

'So you'll let me know?'

'I'll let you know.'

'Right – you know where to find me.'

He had to come right into the office to give himself
enough room, so that he could turn round again to
go out, and then he waddled off with his limp and
his dignity intact.

If you ever see a cat wearing a flat-cap, with a
pint of bitter in one hand and a whippet on a lead
– the odds are it will be Arthur.

We had just finished Sunday lunch when the doorbell rang. Aileen and I were drinking coffee, our

232

little fingers pointed towards the ceiling. Tigger was immersed, or rather asleep, in the *Sunday Times* and Thermal was explaining to a rather bemused sultana how he had been kidnapped and held prisoner by a team of evil builders.

The sultana was ageing fast and I was worried about him – his blood sugar seemed to be a bit on the low side.

The doorbell sounded once more. Who could it be? It wasn't Arthur – he couldn't reach.

There was only one way to find out, and since Aileen seemed to have gone deaf I pulled myself to my feet and went out into the hall.

It was a little girl. She was about six years old and she held a small white kitten in her arms. He was wearing a ginger wig that had been designed for a much taller kitten altogether – I think he had stolen it.

And yet the tip of each ear was a matching ginger, as was the tip of the tail that oozed like toothpaste from between the girl's fingers – perhaps I had misjudged him.

There were tears in the little girl's eyes and the dam was about to burst.

'Will you have my kitten – he's going to be killed.'

You don't get many opening lines like that, and I found myself responding with the most inadequate of replies.

'Is it?'

The kitten nodded and turned his head away – it was all too much for him.

'My daddy's allergic to cats and he's going to have him put down.'

The kitten took a deep breath, swallowed hard and bit its bottom lip.

From down below Patrick's unmistakable voice floated over the hedge.

'And they've got a Dobermann Pinscher – it'll have its head off, so it will.'

Aileen appeared at my shoulder. 'What's happening?'

The girl held the strange little kitten out towards her and Aileen bent forwards until she was almost rubbing noses with it. The kitten blinked.

'Uncle Patrick said you would give him a home. He said you were very kind to kittens.'

'Let me hold him.'

She took him in her arms and cuddled him, then pressed his little body to her face.

'He's just like silk – feel him.' I felt him – he was just like silk. 'Come on in,' she said to the girl and they went in.

'Thank you – thank you very much,' I shouted down to Patrick, 'that's all we needed.'

'Don't mention it, Deric, I know you'll do the right thing.'

I wasn't sure what the right thing was. We were becoming knee deep in cats and I had more or less promised the first vacancy to Arthur.

Aileen had taken the pair of them into her study and was telling the girl that she could come and see the kitten whenever she came over to Patrick's.

'He'll still know me, won't he?'

'Of course he will.'

As soon as she had said a tearful goodbye, Thermal and Tigger wandered in to see what all the fuss was about. Thermal wasn't all that impressed.

'Not much to him, is there?'

Tigger thought he was beautiful. That's how her kitten would have looked – had it lived.

'What shall we call him?' Aileen asked.

'How about Patrick's Revenge?' I suggested, but Thermal didn't seem to agree. He strolled over to have a closer look.

'Thermal's a good strong name – put him down and let's see what he's made of.'

Aileen put him down and he went off like a rocket – straight for Thermal's throat. The element of surprise more than made up for the difference in weight, size and experience, and within seconds Thermal found himself trapped under the television set with an ounce and a half of fur, teeth and claws pounding away at his undercarriage.

He belted it and the kitten rolled over and came again. Thermal jumped up on the desk and the growling ball of fluff bit the carpet in frustration. Tigger moved in as peacemaker – the woman's touch.

The kitten went for her and ran straight through the stiff left jab that had sat Denton on his bottom.

'I wonder what sort it is?' Aileen wanted to know.

'I think it's a civet,' I told her as Tigger shot out of the study with the kitten fastened to her back as though it had been born to ride side-saddle.

They ran straight into Arthur who was coming in to explain how he'd missed his lunch and could he have it now please.

The kitten fell off as the cats collided, but he didn't even stop to adjust his wig – he went straight for Arthur's twisted tail and that was where he made his big mistake.

Arthur might be a cripple, but he was a big strong cripple and he had kittens like this one for breakfast. He simply sat on it.

As this kamikaze kitten skidded in for the kill, he just shifted himself slightly, patted it with his paw and sat on it – it went right underneath him and only its head came out the other side, eyeballs bulging as though it had been run over by a tram.

'We can't keep this one,' I said to Aileen.

'Oh yes we can – I'm going to train it.'

'You're going to need a stool and a whip.'

'Whatever – just give me a week.'

She sucked it out from under Arthur's bum and carried it off to her study. It stared back at us blankly from over her shoulder and wondered why all the lights had gone out.

The rest of us had a meeting and Thermal appointed himself as official union spokesman.

'*It's not stopping, is it?*'

I tried to explain that it was only here on a Youth Opportunities Scheme and it wasn't going to put either of them out of a job.

Tigger would still be literary assistant to Aileen,

and Thermal could have his job as chief food-tester and general charger-about for as long as he wanted.

There was a murmur of discontent and the chief spokesman grunted.

'*You shouldn't take in strange kittens.*'

'I took you in.'

'*That was different – I was cute.*'

'He'll be all right when he's settled down.'

'*It's a she actually – I had a look when we were wrestling.*'

Patrick had certainly got his own back on me – he must have known what a little hooligan it was. But Aileen wanted the kitten and she thought she could civilize it.

But if *she* couldn't – I knew who could.

I knelt down and stroked the broad black back. It arched under my fingers like that of a small camel.

'Excuse me, Arthur – could I have a word with you?' I slipped my arm around his shoulder. 'About that vacancy . . . When can you move in?'

The End!

Tailpiece

The kitten stayed, Arthur moved in and Tigger set about organizing a playschool. Thermal went off in a huff. It was only a short huff – he was back by tea-time. The cats always had fish on a Friday and he wouldn't have missed it for the world. It was a legacy from the old days when my seven-year-old daughter Sally had picked up Ronald, her three-week-old kitten, and asked me, 'How do you know he's not a Catholic?'

The vet told me that we were now the proud owners of a Turkish Van cat.

'They can be little sods when they're kittens.'
'Do they grow out of it?'
'Some do – others grow up into much bigger sods.'

He grew out of it with a big push from Arthur and a little nudge from Aileen. Every time he went berserk either Arthur sat on him or Aileen smacked his nose and then one night he sat down and had a deep think. The prospect of spending his entire life with a curvature of the spine and a sore nose featured high on the agenda and he came to the conclusion that there might be more to life than this.

Thermal revelled in his role as head of the household.